T0029493

Python®
Essentials

by John C. Shovic, PhD,
and Alan Simpson

for
dummies®
A Wiley Brand

Python® Essentials For Dummies®

Published by: **John Wiley & Sons, Inc.**, 111 River Street, Hoboken, NJ 07030-5774, www.wiley.com

Copyright © 2024 by John Wiley & Sons, Inc., Hoboken, New Jersey

Published simultaneously in Canada

For general information on our other products and services, please contact our Customer Care Department within the U.S. at 877-762-2974, outside the U.S. at 317-572-3993, or fax 317-572-4002. For technical support, please visit https://hub.wiley.com/community/support/dummies.

Wiley publishes in a variety of print and electronic formats and by print-on-demand. Some material included with standard print versions of this book may not be included in e-books or in print-on-demand. If this book refers to media such as a CD or DVD that is not included in the version you purchased, you may download this material at http://booksupport.wiley.com. For more information about Wiley products, visit www.wiley.com.

Library of Congress Control Number: 2024934008

ISBN 978-1-394-26347-9 (pbk); ISBN 978-1-394-26348-6 (ebk); ISBN 978-1-394-26349-3 (ebk)

SKY10072503_041324

Contents at a Glance

Table of Contents

Introduction

The Python language is becoming more and more popular, and in 2017 it became the most popular language in the world according to IEEE Spectrum. The power of Python is real.

Python is the number-one language because it's easy to learn and use, due partly to its simplified syntax and natural-language flow but also to the amazing user community and the breadth of applications available.

About This Book

This book is a reference manual to guide you through the process of learning the essentials of Python. If you're looking to learn a little about a lot of exciting things, this is the book for you. It gives you an introduction to the topics that you'll need to explore more deeply.

This is a hands-on book, with examples and code throughout. You'll enter the code, run it, and then modify it to do what you want.

In this book, we take you through the basics of the Python language in small, easy-to-understand steps.

Foolish Assumptions

We assume that you know how to use a computer in a basic way. If you can turn on the computer and use a mouse, you're ready for this book. We assume that you don't know how to program yet, although you will have some skills in programming after reading this book.

Icons Used in This Book

What's a *For Dummies* book without icons pointing you in the direction of truly helpful information that's sure to speed you along your way? Here we briefly describe each icon we use in this book.

The Tip icon points out helpful information that's likely to make your job easier.

The Remember icon marks a generally interesting and useful fact — something you may want to remember for later use.

The Warning icon highlights lurking danger. When we use this icon, we're telling you to pay attention and proceed with caution.

Where to Go from Here

You can start the book anywhere, but here are a couple of hints. If you're brand-new to Python, start with Chapter 1. If you already have some Python experience and you want to learn how to work with bigger chunks of code, head to Chapter 8. For anything else, turn to the Table of Contents or the Index and you'll find what you need.

Chapter **1**

Starting with Python

B ecause you're reading this chapter, you probably realize that Python is a great language to know if you're looking for a good job in programming, or if you want to expand your existing programming skills into exciting cutting-edge technologies such as artificial intelligence (AI), machine learning (ML), data science, or robotics, or even if you're just building apps in general. So we're not going to try to sell you on Python. It sells itself.

Our approach leans heavily toward the hands-on. A common failure in many programming tutorials is that they already assume you're a professional programmer in some language, and they skip over things they assume you already know.

This book is different in that we *don't* assume that you're already programming in Python or some other language. We *do* assume that you can use a computer and understand basics such as files and folders.

We also assume you're not up for settling down in an easy chair in front of the fireplace to read page after page of theoretical stuff about Python, like some kind of boring novel. You don't have that much free time to kill. So we're going to get right into it and focus on *doing*, hands-on, because that's the only way most of us learn. We've never seen anyone read a book about Python and then sit at a computer and write Python like a pro. Human brains don't work that way. We learn through practice and repetition, and that requires being hands-on.

Why Python Is Hot

We promised we weren't going to spend a bunch of time trying to sell you on Python, and that's not our intent here. But we would like to talk briefly about *why* it's so hot.

Here are the main reasons cited for Python's current popularity:

- Python is relatively easy to learn.
- Everything you need to learn (and do) in Python is free.
- Python offers more ready-made tools for current hot technologies such as data science, machine learning, artificial intelligence, and robotics than most other languages.

Choosing the Right Python

There are different *versions* of Python out roaming the world, prompting many a beginner to wonder things such as

- Why are there different versions?
- How are they different?
- Which one should I learn?

All good questions, and we'll start with the first. A version is kind of like a car year. You can go out and buy a 1968 Ford Mustang, a 1990 Ford Mustang, a 2019 Ford Mustang, or a 2020 Ford Mustang. They're all Ford Mustangs. The only difference is that the one with the highest year number is the most current Ford Mustang. That Mustang is different from the older models in that it has some improvements based on experience with earlier models, as well as features current with the times.

Programming languages (and most other software products) work the same way. But as a rule, we don't ascribe year numbers to them because they're not released on a yearly basis. They're released whenever they're released. The principle is the same, though. The version with the highest number is the newest, most recent model, sporting improvements based on experience with earlier versions, as well as features relevant to the current times.

In this book, we focus on versions of Python that are current in late 2023 from Python 3.11 and higher. Don't worry about version differences after the first and second digits. Version 3.11.1 is similar enough to version 3.11.2 that version differences aren't important, especially to a beginner. Most of what's in Python is the same across all recent versions. So you need not worry about investing time in learning a version that is or will soon be obsolete.

Tools for Success

Now we need to start getting your computer set up so that you can learn, and do, Python hands-on. For one, you'll need a good Python interpreter and editor. The *editor* lets you type the code, and the *interpreter* lets you run that code. When you run (or execute) code, you're telling the computer to "do whatever my code tells you to do."

The term *code* refers to anything written in a programming language to provide instructions to a computer. The term *coding* is often used to describe the act of writing code. A code editor is an app that lets you type code, in much the same way an app such as Microsoft Word or Apple Pages helps you type regular, plain-English text.

Just as there are many brands of toothpaste, soap, and shampoo in the world, there are many brands of code editors that work well with Python. There isn't a right one or a wrong one, a good one or a bad one, a best one or a worst one. Just a lot of different products that basically do the same thing but vary slightly in their approach and what that editor's creators think is good.

If you've already started learning Python and are happy with whatever you've been using, you're welcome to continue using that and ignore our suggestions. If you're just getting started with this stuff, we suggest you use VS Code, because it's an excellent, free learning environment.

Installing Python and VS Code

The editor we recommend and will be using in this book is called Visual Studio Code, officially. But most often, it is spoken or written as *VS Code*. The main reasons why it's our favorite follow:

>> It is an excellent editor for learning coding.

>> It is an excellent editor for writing code professionally and is used by millions of professional programmers and developers.

>> It's relatively easy to learn and use.

>> It works pretty much the same on Windows, Mac, and Linux.

>> It's free.

>> It integrates beautifully with GitHub Copilot, so you can use modern, generative AI to speed both learning and actual coding.

To use VS Code as your editor for learning and doing Python, you need to download and install Python, VS Code, and a VS Code extension. With luck, you already have some experience working with apps, so this won't be difficult. You will have to follow onscreen instructions as you go along. If faced with any choices you're not sure about along the way, you can just choose the default (suggested) option. Here are the steps to download and install Python and VS Code:

1. **Use any web browser to browse to** www.python.org.

2. **Click Download and, if asked to select a version, choose the suggested stable version.**

3. **Open the folder to which you downloaded Python and double-click the icon for the file you downloaded to install Python.**

   You can just follow the onscreen instructions, and accept any suggested defaults, during the installation process.

4. **Browse to** https://code.visualstudio.com/ **and download the current version of VS Code for your operating system.**

5. **Open the folder to which you downloaded Visual Studio code, double-click the icon for the downloaded file, and follow the onscreen instructions to install VS Code.**

After VS Code is installed, you should be able to start it like any other app in your system. In Windows, click Start and look around on the Start menu for Visual Studio Code icon. On a Mac, you should be able to find it in your Applications folder, or Launchpad.

Installing the Python extension

To use VS Code for Python coding, you need to install the VS Code Python extension for Python. When you open VS Code, you will see some icons listed down the left side of the window. Placing the mouse cursor over any icon reveals its name. Click the Extensions icon, shown in Figure 1-1, and then enter **Python** in the Search box at the top of the Extensions panel. Click the Install button with the Python extension from Microsoft (see Figure 1-1).

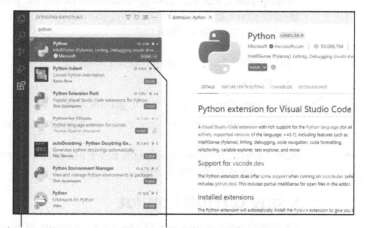

Extensions icon   Install the Python extension from Microsoft

FIGURE 1-1: Obtaining the Python extension in VS Code.

When you've finished installing the Python extension, you might notice that both Python and Pylance were added as extensions to VS Code. Don't worry; that's normal. Pylance just gives you some additional capabilities that make it easier to learn and write Python code within the VS Code editor. To ensure that the extension is activated, exit VS Code and then restart it.

Letting AI write your Python code

Modern generative AI is perfectly capable of writing Python code for you. It's not as simple as commanding it to "Write a Python app that will make me a billionaire," however. It doesn't work that way — yet. Unfortunately. You need to break things down into smaller chunks, and probably use accurate tech terminology, too. In other words, you still have to learn enough Python to be able to write your AI prompts accurately. Virtually all of these prompts — no matter which AI service you use — will start with "Write python code for . . ." because AI can do a lot of things. If you don't tell it, specifically, that you want it to write Python code, you might get no code, HTML, JavaScript, or whatever. So just make sure you understand that, first and foremost.

As we write this in late 2023, generative AI is still fairly new and evolving rapidly. We can't make any promises in terms of pricing or availability. Those things are likely to change often over the coming years, and competing businesses jockey for position and market share. But as of this writing, you can prompt the following AI services to write Python code:

>> ChatGPT (https://chat.openai.com)

>> Claude (https://claude.ai)

>> Google Bard (https://bard.google.com)

>> Microsoft Copilot (https://copilot.microsoft.com)

Most of these tools are free (right now), but again, we can't make any promises about the future.

Using GitHub Copilot

GitHub Copilot is another AI tool that's capable of writing code for you. It's based on OpenAI's GPT-4, like ChatGPT. However, it's specifically geared toward working with code and integrates directly into VS Code. You're certainly not *required* to use GitHub Copilot to learn Python or use this book, but you might find that it really helps your learning process. As we write this book, GitHub is offering Copilot for free to students. It offers some paid plans, too, starting at $10 a month. To use Copilot, you need to sign up for GitHub and purchase (or request) access to Copilot. Again, this tool is so new that any instructions we give here are subject to change. You may need to search Google or YouTube for *use Copilot with VS Code* to find the most up-to-date instructions. Basically, here's how it works:

1. **If you don't already have a GitHub account, go to** https://github.com **and create an account.**

   Make sure you know your GitHub username and password, because you'll need them to set up your account.

2. **Open VS Code if it isn't already open.**

3. **Click Extensions in the left column, and then enter** Copilot **in the Search box to search for Copilot.**

   A list of Copilot extensions appears.

4. **Click the Install button at the right of the plain-old GitHub Copilot extension (not "Copilot Labs" or any of the others that appear), as shown in Figure 1-2.**

Extensions icon   Install GitHub Copilot

FIGURE 1-2: The GitHub Copilot extension in VS Code.

You'll see some instructions and tips on a pane to the right. You need not do anything with those right now, though. Near the lower-left corner of VS Code, you should see an avatar icon for Accounts (see Figure 1-3). Click that icon and choose Sign In with GitHub to Use GitHub Copilot. Follow the on-screen instructions to sign into your GitHub account and set up Copilot. But remember: Setting up a Copilot account isn't a requirement, just an option. So don't feel you have to complete the process of purchasing Copilot right now. But if you do add Copilot as an extension, you should see its name under Installed Extensions whenever you're viewing extensions in VS Code.

Also, near the lower-right corner of the screen, you'll see a tiny Copilot icon (also shown in Figure 1-3). You can click that icon at any time to deactivate Copilot if you feel it's in your way while learning. Click it again to activate Copilot whenever you're ready.

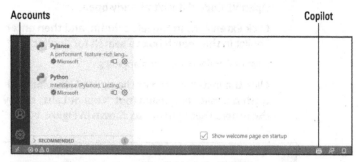

FIGURE 1-3: The Accounts and Copilot icons in VS Code.

The simple tasks you've completed in this chapter will serve you well through your learning process, as well as your professional programming after you've mastered the basics. Head on over to Chapter 2, and we'll delve a bit deeper into Python and using the tools you now have available on your computer.

Chapter **2**

Using Interactive Mode, Getting Help, and Writing Apps

After you've installed VS Code, covered in the previous chapter, you're ready to start digging deeper into writing Python code. In this chapter, we take you briefly through the interactive, help, and code-editing features of VS Code. You're probably anxious to get started on more advanced topics such as data science, artificial intelligence, robotics, or whatever, but learning those topics will be easier if you have a good understanding of the many tools available to you — and the skills to use them.

Using Python's Interactive Mode

One way to get some practical, hands-on experience with using Python is to just start typing some commands interactively. The Terminal pane in VS Code is a great place to type Python code. So in this chapter, that's where you'll start.

Opening Terminal

To use Python interactively with VS Code, follow these steps:

1. **Open VS Code.**
2. **Choose View ⇨ Terminal from the VS Code menu bar.**
3. **If the word *Terminal* isn't highlighted or underlined at the top of the pane, click Terminal (circled in Figure 2-1).**

PROBLEMS	OUTPUT	DEBUG CONSOLE	TERMINAL

PS C:\Users\Alan> █

FIGURE 2-1: The Terminal pane in VS Code.

Going into the Python Interpreter

Whichever command gives you the Python version will also take you to a Python interpreter, where you can enter Python code directly. You'll know you're in the right place when you see the prompt change to three greater-than signs (›››). To get to the command prompt now, enter whichever python command worked for you before, without --version. For example, type just **python** (or just **python3**, or just **py**) and nothing else; then press Enter:

```
python
```

REMEMBER

When we, or anyone else, says "enter the command," that means you have to type the command and then press Enter. Nothing happens until you press Enter. So if you just type the command and wait for something to happen, you'll be waiting for a long, long time. You should see some information about the Python version you're using and the ››› prompt, which represents the Python interpreter.

Entering commands

Entering commands in the Python interpreter is the same as typing them anywhere else. You must type the command correctly and then press Enter. If you spell something wrong in the command, you will likely see an error message, which is just the interpreter telling you it doesn't understand what you mean. But don't worry; you can't break anything. For example, suppose you type the command

```
howdy
```

After you press Enter, you'll see some techie gibberish that is trying to tell you that the interpreter doesn't know what "howdy" means, so it can't do anything. Nothing has broken. You're just back to another >>> prompt, where you can try again, as shown in Figure 2-2.

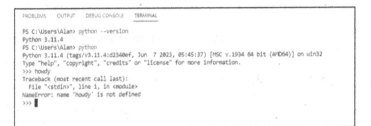

FIGURE 2-2: Python doesn't know what *howdy* means.

Using Python's built-in help

One of the prompts in Figure 2-2 mentions that you can type **help** as a command in the Python interpreter. Note that you don't type the quotation marks, just the word *help* (and then press Enter, as always). This time you see

```
Type help() for interactive help, or help(object)
    for help about object.
```

Now the interpreter is telling you to type **help** followed by an empty pair of parentheses, or type **help** with a specific word in parentheses (*object* is the example given). Make sure you press Enter after typing your command. Go ahead and enter the following:

```
help()
```

Note that the line does not have spaces. After you press Enter, the screen provides some information about using Python's interactive help.

Seeing `help>` at the bottom of the window tells you that you're no longer in the operating system shell or the Python interpreter (which always shows > > >) but are now in a new area that provides help. As described on the screen, you can enter the name of any module, keyword, or topic to get help with that term. As a beginner, you might not need help with specifics right at the moment. But it's good to know that the help is there if you need it.

For example, Python uses certain keywords that have special meaning in the language. To get a list of those keywords, just type the following at the `help>` prompt:

```
keywords
```

After you press Enter, you see a list of keywords, as shown in Figure 2-3.

```
PROBLEMS    OUTPUT    DEBUG CONSOLE    TERMINAL

help> keywords

Here is a list of the Python keywords.  Enter any keyword to get more help.

False          class          from           or
None           continue       global         pass
True           def            if             raise
and            del            import         return
as             elif           in             try
assert         else           is             while
async          except         lambda         with
await          finally        nonlocal       yield
break          for            not

help> █
```

FIGURE 2-3: Keyword help.

All the technical jargon in the help text will leave the average beginner flummoxed. But as you learn about new concepts in Python, realize that you can use the interactive help for guidance as needed.

TIP

If you see --More-- at the bottom of the text that isn't a prompt where you type commands. Instead, it just lets you know that there is more text, perhaps several pages' worth. Press the spacebar or Enter to see it. Every time you see -- More --, you can press the spacebar or Enter to get to the next page. Eventually you'll get back to the `help>` prompt. If you want to quit rather than keep scrolling, press Q.

Exiting interactive help

To leave the Python prompt and get back to the operating system, type **exit()** and press Enter. Note that if you make a mistake, such as forgetting the parentheses, you'll get some help on the screen. For example, if you type **exit** and press Enter, you'll see

```
Use exit() or Ctrl-Z plus Return to exit.
```

Don't be thrown by "Ctrl-Z" versus "Ctrl+Z" for keypress combinations; they both mean the same thing.

TIP

You'll know you've exited the Python interpreter when you see the operating system prompt rather than >>> at the end of the Terminal pane.

Searching for specific help topics online

Python's built-in help is useful when you know the exact terminology and concept you want to look up. But that's often tough for beginners. When you're online, you may be better off searching the web for help. If you're looking for videos, start at www.youtube.com; if not, https://stackoverflow.com is a good place to ask questions and search for help. And, of course, there's always Google, Bing, and other search engines.

Regardless of what you use to search, remember to start your search with the word *python*. A lot of programming languages share similar concepts and keywords, so if you don't specify the Python language in your search request, there's no telling what **REMEMBER** kinds of results you may get.

Creating a Folder for Your Python Code

In this section, you create a folder to store all the Python code that you write in this book so that it's all together in one place and easy to find when you need it. You can put this folder anywhere you like and name it whatever you like.

In Windows, you can navigate to the folder that will contain the new folder. (Alan uses OneDrive, but you can use Desktop, Documents, or any other folder.) Right-click an empty place in the folder and then choose New Folder (Mac) or New ⇨ Folder

(Windows). Type the folder name and press Enter. To follow along with the examples in this chapter, name your folder Python Essentials.

Typing, Editing, and Debugging Python Code

Most likely, you'll write the vast majority of code in an editor. As you probably know, an *editor* enables you to type and edit text. Code is text. The editor in VS Code is set up for typing and editing code, so you may hear it referred to as a *code editor.*

Because people tend to organize code into folders (as we suggest you do for this chapter's examples), your first step is to open the folder that contains your code in your editor. There are a few ways to do that. If this is your first time, follow these steps:

1. **Open VS Code using the Start menu in Windows or Launchpad on a Mac.**

2. **Click File ⇨ Open Folder from VS Code's menu bar, navigate to the folder's location, click the name of the folder you want to open, and click Select Folder.**

    The name of the currently open folder appears near the top of the Explorer pane at the left side of the VS Code window.

TIP

Each Python code file you create will be a plain-text file with a .py filename extension. We suggest that you keep any files you create for this book in that Python Essentials folder (see the previous section for how to create that folder). You should be able to see your Python Essentials folder anytime VS Code and your Python 3 workspace are open.

To create a .py file at any time, follow these steps:

1. **If you haven't already done so, open VS Code and your Python Essentials folder.**

2. **If the Explorer pane isn't open, click the Explorer icon near the top-left of VS Code.**

3. **To create a file in your Python Essentials folder, click New File to the right of the folder name.**

4. **Type the filename with the** .py **extension (hello.py for this first one) and press Enter.**

The new file opens and you can see its name in the tab on the right. The larger area below the tab is the editor, where you type the Python code. The filename also appears under the Python Essentials folder name in the Explorer pane, because that's where it's stored.

Writing Python code

Now that you have a .py file open, you can use it to write some Python code. As is typical when learning a new programming language, you'll start by typing a simple Hello World program. Here are the steps:

1. **Click just to the right of line 1 in the editing area.**

2. **Type the following:**

```
print("Hello World")
```

As you're typing, you may notice text appearing on the screen. That text is *IntelliSense text,* which detects what you're typing and shows you some information about that keyword. Exactly how much information you see depends on whether you're using GitHub Copilot. But you don't have to do anything with that — just keep typing.

3. **Press Enter after you've typed the line.**

The new line of code is displayed on the screen. You may also notice a few other changes, as shown in Figure 2-4:

» The Explorer icon sports a dot, or perhaps a circled 1, indicating that you currently have one unsaved change.

» The hello.py name in the tab displays a dot, which indicates that the file has unsaved changes.

Saving your code

Code you type in VS Code is not saved automatically. There are two ways to deal with that. One is to try to remember to save anytime you make a change that's worth saving. The easiest way to do that is to choose File ⇨ Save from VS Code's menu bar or press Ctrl+S in Windows or ⌘+S on a Mac.

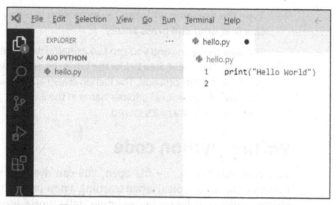

FIGURE 2-4: The hello.py file contains some Python code and has unsaved changes.

We prefer the second method, which is to use AutoSave to automatically save changes we make. To enable Auto Save, choose File ⇨ Auto Save from VS Code's menu bar. The next time you open the File menu, you'll see a check mark next to Auto Save, which tells you that that Auto Save is turned on. To turn off Auto Save, just choose File ⇨ Auto Save again. The file is saved automatically as you make changes.

Running Python in VS Code

To test your Python code in VS Code, you need to run it. The easiest way to run it is to right-click the file's name (hello.py in this example) and choose Run Python File in Terminal.

If prompted to choose a Python interpreter, just choose the one you downloaded and installed in Chapter 1. Typically, it will be marked as Recommended. If you get stuck, choose View ⇨ Command Palette from VS Code's menu bar. Type **python** and then click Python: Select Interpreter. Choose the Recommended option. Then try running hello.py again as described in the previous paragraph.

The Terminal pane opens along the bottom of the VS Code window. You'll see a command prompt followed by a comment to run the code in the Python interpreter (python.exe). Below that, you'll see the output of the program: the words *Hello World*, in this example, and then another prompt, as shown in Figure 2-5. This app is not the most exciting one in the world, but at least now you know how to write, save, and execute a Python program in VS Code, a skill you'll be using often as you continue through this book and throughout your Python programming career.

```
PROBLEMS    OUTPUT    DEBUG CONSOLE    TERMINAL

PS C:\Users\Alan\OneDrive\AIO Python> & C:/Users/Alan/AppData/L
Hello World
PS C:\Users\Alan\OneDrive\AIO Python>
```

FIGURE 2-5: Output from hello.py.

Learning simple debugging

REMEMBER

When you're first learning to write code, you're bound to make a lot of mistakes. Realize that mistakes are no big deal — you won't break or destroy anything. The code just won't work as expected.

Before you attempt to run some code, you might see several screen indications of an error in your code:

>> The number of errors in the file will appear in red next to the filename in the Explorer pane at the left side of the screen.

>> The total number of errors or warnings will appear near the lower-left corner of the VS Code app window.

>> The bad code will have a wavy underline.

In Figure 2-6, we typed PRINT in all uppercase, which is not allowed in Python. Python is case sensitive, and the correct command is in all lowercase letters: print. Remember that when we show a command to type in lowercase, you have to type it in lowercase, too.

To run the file in Terminal, you must fix the error. In the example shown in Figure 2-6, we would just replace *PRINT* with *print*, and then save the change (unless we've turned on Auto Save). Then we can right-click and choose Run Python File in Terminal to run the corrected code.

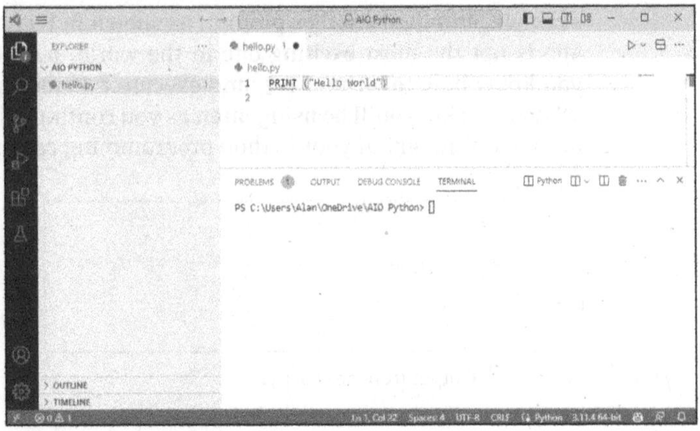

FIGURE 2-6: PRINT is typed incorrectly in hello.py.

Closing a file

When you're finished working with a particular program or file in VS Code, you can easily close it. Just click the X next to the filename in its tab, or choose File ⇨ Close Editor. Whenever the Explorer pane is open, the name of the file will still be visible in the Explorer pane at the left side of the VS Code window. Just click the filename whenever you want to reopen the file in the editor.

That should be enough to get you set up to learn, and run, Python on your computer. I won't spend a lot of time on VS Code here, because those aren't Python, per se. They're tools used by programmers working in many languages. There are many free tutorials for using VS Code with Python on YouTube and elsewhere. So feel free to learn what you can, as convenient, from those other sources as you learn the Python language. Now come on over to Chapter 3 and let's get deeper into it.

Chapter **3**
Python Elements and Syntax

M any programming languages focus on things that the computer does and how it does them rather than on the way humans think and work. This one simple fact makes most programming languages difficult for most people to learn. Python, however, is based on the philosophy that a programming language should be geared more toward how humans think, work, and communicate than to what happens inside the computer. The Zen of Python is the perfect example of that human orientation, so we start this chapter with that topic.

The Zen of Python

The *Zen of Python*, shown in Figure 3-1, is a list of the guiding principles for the design of the Python language. These principles are hidden in an *Easter egg*, which is a term for something in a programming language or an app that's not easy to find and that's an inside joke to people who have learned enough of the language or app to be able to find the Easter egg. To get to the Easter egg, follow these steps:

1. **Open VS Code in the usual manner on your computer (through Launchpad on a Mac or the Start menu on Windows) and then open your** `Python Essentials` **folder.**

   TIP

   If you don't have a `Python Essentials` folder yet, turn to Chapter 2 for information on how to create that.

2. **If the Terminal pane isn't open, choose View ⇨ Terminal from the VS Code menu bar.**

3. **Type** python **and press Enter to get to the Python prompt (>>>). If you get an error, on a Mac type** python3, **or in Windows, type** py.

4. **At the** >>> **prompt, type** import this **and press Enter.**

   The list of aphorisms appears. You may have to scroll up and down or make the Terminal pane taller to see them all. The aphorisms are somewhat tongue in cheek in their philosophical rhetoric, but the general idea they express is to always try to make the code more human readable than machine readable.

```
PROBLEMS    OUTPUT    DEBUG CONSOLE    TERMINAL

PS C:\Users\Alan\OneDrive\AIO Python> python
Python 3.11.4 (tags/v3.11.4:d2340ef, Jun  7 2023, 05:45:37) [MSC v.1934 64 bit (AMD64)] on win32
Type "help", "copyright", "credits" or "license" for more information.
>>> import this
The Zen of Python, by Tim Peters

Beautiful is better than ugly.
Explicit is better than implicit.
Simple is better than complex.
Complex is better than complicated.
Flat is better than nested.
Sparse is better than dense.
Readability counts.
Special cases aren't special enough to break the rules.
Although practicality beats purity.
Errors should never pass silently.
Unless explicitly silenced.
In the face of ambiguity, refuse the temptation to guess.
There should be one-- and preferably only one --obvious way to do it.
Although that way may not be obvious at first unless you're Dutch.
Now is better than never.
Although never is often better than *right* now.
If the implementation is hard to explain, it's a bad idea.
If the implementation is easy to explain, it may be a good idea.
Namespaces are one honking great idea -- let's do more of those!
>>> []
```

FIGURE 3-1: The Zen of Python.

The Zen of Python is sometimes referred to as *PEP 20*, where *PEP* is an acronym for *Python enhancement proposals*. The 20 perhaps refers to the 20 Zen of Python principles, only 19 of which have been written down. We all get to wonder about or make up our own final principle.

Introducing Object-Oriented Programming

At the risk of getting too technical or computer science-y, we should mention that there are different approaches to designing languages. Perhaps the most successful and widely used model is *object-oriented programming*, or OOP, which is a design philosophy that tries to mimic the real world in the sense that it consists of objects with properties as well as methods (actions) that those objects perform.

Python is very much an object-oriented language. The core language consists of controls (in the form of words) that allow you to control all different kinds of objects — in your own and other peoples' programs. However, you need to learn the core language first so that when you're ready to start using other peoples' objects, you know how to do so. Similarly, after you know how to drive one car, you pretty much know how to drive them all. You don't have to worry about renting a car only to discover that the accelerator is on the roof, the steering wheel on the floor, and you have to use voice commands rather than a brake to slow it down. The basic skill of driving applies to all cars.

Discovering Why Indentations Count, Big Time

In terms of the basic style of writing code, the one feature that really makes Python different from many other languages is that it uses indentations rather than parentheses and curly braces and such to indicate blocks, or chunks, of code. We don't assume that you're familiar with other languages, so don't worry if that statement means nothing to you.

The rules are opposite in Python because it doesn't use curly braces or any other special characters to mark the beginning and end of a block of code. The indentations themselves mark those. So those indentations aren't optional — they are required, and they have a considerable effect on how the code runs. As a result, when you read the code (as a human, not as a computer), it's relatively easy to see what's going on, and you're not distracted by a ton of extra quotation marks.

```python
import random
question = input("Ask Magic 8 Ball a question")
answer = random.randint(1, 8)
if answer == 1:
    print("It is certain")
elif answer == 2:
    print("Outlook good")
elif answer == 3:
    print("You may rely on it")
elif answer == 4:
    print("Ask again later")
elif answer == 5:
    print("Concentrate and ask again")
elif answer == 6:
    print("Reply hazy, try again")
elif answer == 7:
    print("My reply is no")
elif answer == 8:
    print("My sources say no")
else:
    print("That's not a question")
print("The end")
```

TIP

You may have noticed at the top of the Python code the line that starts with import. Lines that start with import are common in Python, and you'll see why in the next section.

Using Python Modules

One of the secrets to Python's success is that it's composed of a simple, clean, core language. That's the part you need to learn first. In addition to that core language, many, many modules are available that you can grab for free and access from your own code. These modules are also written in the core language, but you don't need to see that or even know it because you can access all the power of the modules from the basic core language.

Most modules are for some a specific application such as science or artificial intelligence or working with dates and time or . . . whatever. The beauty of using modules is that other people spent a lot of time creating, testing, and fine-tuning that module so that you don't have to. You simply import the module into your own Python file, and use the module's capabilities as instructed in the module's documentation.

The sample Magic 8 Ball program in the previous section starts with this line:

```
import random
```

The core Python language has nothing built into it to generate a random number. Although we could figure out a way to make a random number generator, we don't need to because someone has figured out how to do it and has made the code freely available. Starting your program with import random tells the program that you want to use the capabilities of the random number module to generate a random number. Then, later in the program, you generate a random number between 1 and 8 with this line of code:

```
answer = random.randint(1, 8)
```

As mentioned earlier, in your own Python code, you must import a module before you can access its capabilities. The syntax for doing so is

```
import modulename [as alias]
```

Code written in a generic format like that, with some parts in italic and some in square brackets, is sometimes called a *syntax chart* because it's not showing you, literally, what to type. Rather, it's showing the syntax (format) of the code. Here is how information is presented in such a syntax chart:

» The code is case sensitive, meaning you must type **import** and **as** using all lowercase letters, as shown.

>> Anything in italics is a placeholder for information you should supply in your own code. For example, in your code, you would replace *modulename* with the name of the module you want to import.

>> Anything in square brackets is optional, so you can type the command with or without the part in square brackets.

REMEMBER

You can type the `import` line any place you type Python code: at the Python command prompt (>>>) or in a .py file. In a .py file, always put `import` statements first so that their capabilities are available to the rest of the code.

Chapter **4**

Building Your First Python Application

So, you want to build an application in Python? Whether you want to code a website, analyze data, or create a script to automate something, this chapter gives you the basics you need to get started on your journey. Most people use programming languages like Python to create *application programs.* To create apps, you need to know how to write code inside a code editor.

Like any language, you need to understand the individual words so that you can start building sentences and, finally, the blocks of code that will enable your app to work. First, we walk you through creating an app file in which you will create your code. Then you learn the various data types, operators, and variables, which are the words of the Python language, and then Python syntax.

Opening the Python App File

You'll be using the ever-popular Visual Studio Code (VS Code) editor in this book to learn Python and create Python apps. We assume that you've already set up your learning and development environment, as described in the previous chapters, and know how to open VS Code. To follow along in this chapter, start with these steps:

1. **Use Launchpad on a Mac or the Start menu in Windows to open VS Code, and then choose File ⇨ Open Folder or the Explorer pane in VS Code to open the** Python Essentials **folder you create in Chapter 2.**

   You may notice a new folder named .vscode in with your other files. Don't worry; it's just information used by VS Code, and you can ignore it for now.

2. **If you created the** hello.py **file as described in Chapter 2, click it; otherwise, create it now and then come back here.**

3. **Select all the text on the first line and delete it so that you can start from scratch.**

At this point, hello.py should be open in the editor, as shown in Figure 4-1. If any other tabs are open, close them by clicking the X in each.

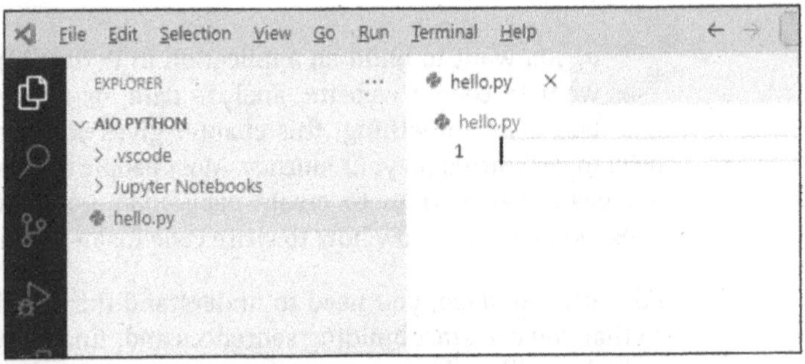

FIGURE 4-1: The hello.py file, open for editing in VS Code.

Typing and Using Python Comments

Before you type any code, start with a programmer's comment. A *programmer's comment* (usually called a *comment* for short) is text in the program that does nothing. Which brings up the question, "If it doesn't *do* anything, why type it in?" As a learner, you can use comments in your code as notes to yourself about what the code is doing. These can help a lot when you're first learning.

However, comments in code aren't strictly for beginners. When working in teams, professionals often use comments to explain to team members what their code is doing. Developers also put comments in their code as notes to themselves so that if they review the code in the future, they can refer to their own notes for reminders on why they did something in the code. Because a comment isn't code, your wording can be anything you want. However, to be identified as a comment, you must do one of the following:

» Start the text with a pound sign (#)

» Enclose the text in triple quotation marks (""" or ' ' ')

```
# This is a Python comment
```

To type a Python comment into your own code:

1. **In VS Code, click next to the 1 under the hello.py tab and type the following:**

   ```
   # This is a Python comment in my first
       Python app.
   ```

2. **Press Enter.**

   The comment you typed appears on line 1. The comment text will be green if you're using the default color theme.

Although you won't use multiline comments just yet, be aware that you can type longer comments in Python by enclosing them in triple quotation marks. These larger comments are sometimes called *docstrings* and often appear at the top of a Python module, function, class, or method definition, which are app building blocks.

You can have an unlimited number of comments in your code. If you're waiting for something to happen after you type a comment . . . don't. When you're working in an editor like this, code doesn't do anything until you run it. Before you start typing code, you need to start with the absolute basics.

Understanding Python Data Types

You deal with written information all the time and probably don't think about the difference between numbers and text. Numbers are amounts, such as 10 or 123.45. Text consists of letters and words. For computers, the big difference is that they can do arithmetic (add, subtract, multiple, divide) with numbers, but not with letters and words.

Numbers

Numbers in Python must start with a number digit, (0–9); a dot (period), which is a decimal point; or a hyphen (-) used as a negative sign for negative numbers. A number can contain only one decimal point. It should not contain letters, spaces, dollar signs, or anything else that isn't part of a normal number.

TIP

If you're worried that the number rules won't let you work with dollar amounts, zip codes, addresses, or anything else, stop worrying. You can store and work with *all* kinds of information, as you'll see shortly.

Integers

An *integer* is any whole number, positive or negative. There is no limit to its size. Numbers such as 0, −1, and 999999999999999 are all perfectly valid integers. From your perspective, an integer is just any valid number that doesn't contain a decimal point.

Floats

A *floating-point number*, often called a *float*, is any valid number that contains a decimal point. Again, there is no size limit: 1.1 and −1.1 and 123456.789012345 are all perfectly valid floats.

If you work with very large scientific numbers, you can put an *e* in a number to indicate the power of 10. For example, 234e1000 is a valid number, and will be treated as a float even if there's no decimal point. If you're familiar with scientific notation, you know 234e3 is 234,000 (replace the *e3* with three zeroes). If you're not familiar with scientific notation, don't worry about it. If you're not using it in your day-to-day work now, chances are you'll never need it in Python either.

Words (strings)

Strings are sort of the opposite of numbers. With numbers, you can add, subtract, multiply, and divide because the numbers represent quantities. Strings are for just about everything else. A name, address, or kind of text you see every day would be a string in Python (and in computers in general). It's called a *string* because it's a string of characters (letters, spaces, punctuation marks, and maybe some numbers). To us, a string usually has some meaning, such as a person's name or address. But computers don't have eyes to see with or brains to think with or any awareness that humans even exist, so to a computer, if a piece of information is not something on which it can do arithmetic, it's just a string of characters.

Unlike numbers, a string must always be enclosed in quotation marks. You can use either double (") or single (') quotation marks. All the following are valid strings:

```
"Hi there, I am a string"
'Hello world'
"123 Oak Tree Lane"
"(267)555-1234"
"18901-3384"
```

Note that it's fine to use numeric characters (0–9) as well as hyphens and dots (periods) in strings. Each is still a string because it's enclosed in quotation marks.

WARNING

A word of caution: If a string contains an apostrophe (single quote), the entire string should be enclosed in double quotation marks like this:

```
"Mary's dog said Woof"
```

Booleans

A third data type in Python isn't exactly a number or a string. It's called a *Boolean* (named after a mathematician named George Boole), and it can be one of two values: True or False.

In Python code, people store `True` and `False` values in *variables* (placeholders in code that we discuss later in this chapter) using a format similar to this:

```
x = True
```

or perhaps this:

```
x = False
```

The *initial cap* is required. In other words, the Boolean values `True` and `False` must be written as shown.

TIP

Working with Python Operators

As we discuss in the preceding section, it helps with Python and computers in general to think of information as being one of the following data types: number, string, or Boolean. You also use computers to *operate* on that information, meaning to do any necessary math or comparisons or searches or whatever to help you find information and organize it in a way that makes sense to you.

Python offers many different *operators* for working with and comparing types of information. Whether you use an operator in your own work depends on the types of apps you develop. For now, it's sufficient just to be aware that they're available.

Arithmetic operators

Arithmetic operators, as the name implies, are for doing arithmetic: addition, subtraction, multiplication, division, and more. Table 4-1 lists Python's arithmetic operators.

TABLE 4-1 **Python's Arithmetic Operators**

Operator	Description	Example
+	Addition	`1 + 1 = 2`
–	Subtraction	`10 - 1 = 9`
*	Multiplication	`3 * 5 = 15`
/	Division	`10 / 5 = 2`

Comparison operators

Computers can make decisions as part of doing their work. But these decisions are not judgment call decisions or anything human like that. These decisions are based on absolute facts that are based on comparisons. The *comparison operators* that Python offers to help you write code that makes decisions are listed in Table 4-2.

TABLE 4-2 Python Comparison Operators

Operator	Meaning
<	Less than
<=	Less than or equal to
>	Greater than
>=	Greater than or equal to
==	Equal to
!=	Not equal to

Boolean operators

The *Boolean operators* work with Boolean values (True or False) and are used to determine whether one or more things is True or False. Table 4-3 summarizes the Boolean operators.

TABLE 4-3 Python Boolean Operators

Operator	Code Example	What It Determines
or	x or y	Either x or y is True
and	x and y	Both x and y are True
not	not x	x is not True

We haven't told you what variables are, so that part of the example may have left you scratching your head. We clear up that part of this business next.

Creating and Using Variables

Variables are a big part of Python and all computer programming languages. A *variable* is simply a placeholder for information that may vary (change).

In your code, a variable is represented by a variable *name* rather than a specific piece of information. Here is another way to think of it. Anytime you buy one or more of some product, the extended price is the unit price times the number of items you bought. In other words:

> Extended Price = Quantity * Unit Price

You can consider Quantity and Unit Price to be variables because no matter what numbers you plug in for Quantity and Unit Price, you get the correct extended price. For example, if you buy three turtle doves for $1.00 apiece, your extended price is $3.00 (3 * $1.00). If you buy two dozen roses for $1.50 apiece, the extended price is $36 because 1.5 * 24 is 36.

Creating valid variable names

In our explanation of variables, we used names like Quantity and Unit Price, and this is fine for a general example. In Python, you can also make up your own variable names, but they must conform to the following rules to be recognized as variable names:

>> The variable name must start with a letter or an underscore (_).

>> After the first character, you can use only letters, numbers, or underscores.

>> Variable names are case sensitive, so after you make up a name, any reference to that variable must use the same uppercase and lowercase letters.

>> Variable names cannot be enclosed in, or contain, single or double quotation marks.

>> The variable name cannot be the same as a Python keyword.

Creating variables in code

To create a variable, you use the following syntax (order of things):

```
variablename = value
```

where *variablename* is the name you make up. You can use *x* or *y*, as people often do in math, but in larger programs, it's a good idea to give your variables more meaningful names, such as quantity or unit_price or sales_tax or user_name, so that you can remember what you're storing in the variable.

The *value* is whatever you want to store in the variable. It can be a number, a string, or a Boolean True or False value or result of a calculation.

The = sign is the *assignment operator* and is so named because it assigns the value (on the right) to the variable (on the left). For example, in the following:

```
x = 10
```

we are storing the number 10 in a variable named x. In other words, we're assigning the value 10 to the x variable.

And here:

```
user_name = "Alan"
```

we're putting the string Alan in a variable named user_name.

Manipulating variables

Much of computer programming revolves around storing values in variables and manipulating that information with operators. Following are some simple examples to help you get the hang of it. If you still have VS Code open with that one comment displayed, follow these steps in the VS Code editor:

1. **Under the line that reads** # *This is a Python comment in my first Python app.*, **type this comment and press Enter:**

```
# This variable contains an integer
```

2. Type the following (don't forget to put a space before and after the = sign) and press Enter:

```
quantity = 10
```

3. Type the following and press Enter:

```
# This variable contains a float
```

4. Type the following (don't type a dollar sign!) and press Enter:

```
unit_price = 1.99
```

5. Type the following and press Enter:

```
# This variable contains the result of
   multiplying quantity times unit price
```

6. Type the following (with spaces around the operators) and press Enter:

```
extended_price = quantity * unit_price
```

7. Type the following and press Enter:

```
# Show the results
```

8. Finally, type this and press Enter:

```
print(extended_price)
```

Your Python app creates some variables, stores some values in them, and calculates a new value, extended_price, based on the contents of the quantity and unit_price variables. The last line displays the contents of the extended_price variable on the screen. Remember, the comments don't *do* anything in the program as it's running. The comments are just notes to yourself about what's going on in the program.

If you made any errors, you may see some wavy lines near errors or stylistic suggestions, such as an extra space or an omitted Enter at the end of a line. When typing code, you must be accurate.

In other words, if the code is wrong, it won't work when you run it. It's as simple as that — no exceptions.

Saving your work

Typing code is like typing other documents on a computer. If you don't save your work, you may not have it the next time you sit down at your computer and go looking for it. So, if you haven't enabled Auto Save on the File menu, as discussed in Chapter 2, choose File ⇨ Save.

Running your Python app in VS Code

Now you can run the app and see if it works. An easy way to do that is to right-click the `hello.py` filename in the Explorer pane and choose Run Python File in Terminal.

If your code is typed correctly, you should see the result, 19.9, in the Terminal pane, as shown in Figure 4-2. The result is the output from `print(extended_price)` in the code, and it's 19.9 because the quantity (10) times the unit price (1.99) is 19.9.

```
PROBLEMS    OUTPUT    DEBUG CONSOLE    TERMINAL

PS C:\Users\Alan\OneDrive\AIO Python> & C:/Users/
19.9
PS C:\Users\Alan\OneDrive\AIO Python>
```

FIGURE 4-2: The 19.9 is the output from `print(extended_price)` in the code.

Suppose your app must calculate the total cost of 14 items that each cost $26.99. Can you think of how to make that happen? You certainly wouldn't need to write a whole new app. Instead, in the code you're working with now, change the value of the quantity variable from 10 to 14. Change the value of the `unitprice` variable to 26.99 (remember, no dollar signs in your number). Here's how the code looks with those changes:

```
# This is a Python comment in my first Python app.
# This variable contains an integer
quantity = 14
# This variable contains a float
```

```
unit_price = 26.99
# This variable contains the result of multiplying
    quantity times unit price
extended_price = quantity * unit_price
# Show some results on the screen.
print(extended_price)
```

Save your work (unless you've turned on AutoSave). Then run the app by right-clicking and choosing Run Python File in Terminal once again — just like the first time. But you should see the correct answer, 377.85999999999996, in the Terminal pane near the bottom of the VS Code window. It doesn't round to pennies and it doesn't even look like a dollar amount. But you need to learn to crawl before you can learn to pole vault, so for now just be happy with getting your apps to run.

Understanding What Syntax Is and Why It Matters

Proper syntax in programming languages is every bit as important as it is in human languages — even more so, in some ways, because when you make a mistake speaking or writing to someone, that other person can usually figure out what you meant by the context of your words. But computers aren't nearly that smart. Computers don't have brains, can't guess your actual meaning based on context, and in fact the concept of context doesn't even exist for computers. So syntax matters even more in programming languages than in human languages.

Looking back at the earliest code in this chapter, note that most of the lines of actual code (not the comments, which start with #) follow this syntax:

```
variablename = value
```

where *variablename* is some name you made up, and *value* is something you are storing in that variable. It works because it's the proper syntax. If you try to do it like this, it won't work:

```
value = variablename
```

For example, the following is the correct way to store the value 10 in a variable named x:

```
x = 10
```

It might seem you could also do it the following way, but it won't work in Python:

```
10 = x
```

If you typed it that way in VS Code, you'd see some wavy underlines beneath the code, indicating that you didn't follow the rules of syntax, and your code can't be executed as written. You can touch the mouse pointer to any code that shows a wavy underline, to see more information about the error.

In Python, a line of code ends with a line break or a semicolon. For example, this is three lines of Python code:

```
first_name = "Alan"
last_name = "Simpson"
print(first_name, last_name)
```

It would also be acceptable to use a semicolon instead of a line break, if you want to put more than one statement on a single line:

```
first_name = "Alan"; last_name = "Simpson"
print(first_name, last_name)
```

Note how the variable names are all lowercase, and the words are separated by an underscore:

```
first_name
last_name
```

REMEMBER

Using all lowercase letters for variable names with words separated by underscores is a *naming convention* in Python. But note that a *convention* is not the same as a *syntax rule*. You could name the variables as follows without breaking any syntax rules:

```
FirstName
LastName
```

So far you've looked at lines of code. There are also *code blocks* where two or more lines of code work together. Here is an example:

```
x = 10
if x == 0:
    print("x is zero")
else:
    print("x is",x)
print("All done")
```

The two equal signs (==) means "is equal to" in Python and is used to compare values to one another to see whether they're equal. That's different from just one equal sign (=), which is the assignment operator for assigning variables.

The first line, x = 10, is just a line of code. Next, the if x == 0 tests to see whether the x variable contains the number 0. If x *does* contain 0, the indented line print("x is zero") executes, and that's what you see on the screen. However, if x does not contain 0, that indented line is skipped and the else: statement executes. The indented line under else:, print("x is",x), executes, but *only* if the x doesn't contain 0. The last line, print("All done!"), executes no matter what, because it's not indented.

REMEMBER

So, as you can see, indentations matter a lot in Python. In the preceding code, only one of the indented lines will execute depending on the value in x. You learn about the specifics of using indentations in your code as you progress through the book. For now, just try to remember that syntax and indentations are important in Python, so you must type carefully when writing code.

This chapter takes you through how to type, save, run, and change an app, save it again, and run it again. Those tasks define what you'll be doing with any kind of software development in any language, so you should practice them until they become second nature. You'll be using these same skills throughout this book as you work your way from beginner to hot-shot 21st-century Python developer.

Chapter **5**

Working with Numbers, Text, and Dates

Computer languages in general, and certainly Python, deal with information in ways that are different from what you may be used to in your everyday life. This idea takes some getting used to. In the computer world, *numbers* are numbers you can add, subtract, multiply, and divide. Python also differentiates between whole numbers (integers) and numbers that contain a decimal point (floats). Words (textual information such as names and addresses) are stored as strings, which is short for "a string of characters." In addition to numbers and strings, there are Boolean values, which can be either True or False.

In real life, we also have to deal with dates and times, which are yet another type of information. Python doesn't have a built-in data type for dates and times, but thankfully, a free module you can import any time works with such information. This chapter is all about taking full advantage of the various Python data types.

Calculating Numbers with Functions

A *function* in Python is similar to a function on a calculator, in that you pass something into the function, and the function passes something back. For example, most calculators and programming languages have a square root function: You provide a number, and they tell you the square root of that number.

Python functions generally have the syntax:

```
variablename = functioname(param[,param])
```

Because most functions return some value, you typically start by defining a variable to store what the function returns. Follow that with the = sign and the function name, followed by a pair of parentheses. Inside the parentheses you may pass one or more values (called *parameters*) to the function.

For example, the abs() function accepts one number and returns the absolute value of that number. If you're not a math nerd, this just means that if you pass it a negative number, it returns that same number as a positive number. If you pass it a positive number, it returns the same number you passed it. In other words, the abs() function simply converts negative numbers to positive numbers.

Here's an example (which you can try out for yourself hands-on at the Python prompt or in a .py file in VS Code):

```
x = -4
y =abs(x)
print(x)
print(y)


-4
4
```

Here, we created a variable named x and assigned it the value -4. Then we created a variable named y and assigned it the absolute value of x using the abs() function. Printing x shows its value, -4, which hasn't changed. Printing y shows 4, the absolute value of x as returned by the abs() function.

Python has many built-in functions for working with numbers, as shown in Table 5-1. Some may not mean much to you if you're not into math in a big way, but don't let that intimidate you. If you don't understand what a function does, chances are it's not doing something relevant to the kind of work you do. But if you're curious, you can always search the web for *python* followed by the function name for more information. For a more extensive list, search for *python 3 built-in functions*.

TABLE 5-1 Some Built-In Python Functions for Numbers

Built-In Function	Purpose
abs(*x*)	Returns the absolute value of number *x* (converts negative numbers to positive).
bin(*x*)	Returns a string representing the value of *x* converted to binary.
float(*x*)	Converts a string or number *x* to the float data type.
format(*x*, *y*)	Returns *x* formatted according to the pattern specified in *y*. This older syntax has been replaced with f-strings in current Python versions.
hex(*x*)	Returns a string containing *x* converted to hexadecimal, prefixed with 0x.
int(*x*)	Converts *x* to the integer data type by truncating (not rounding) the decimal portion and any digits after it.
max(*x*, *y*, *z*, ...)	Takes any number of numeric arguments and returns whichever is the largest.
min(*x*, *y*, *z*, ...)	Takes any number of numeric arguments and returns whichever is the smallest.
round(*x*, *y*)	Rounds the number *x* to *y* number of decimal places.
str(*x*)	Converts the number *x* to the string data type.
type(*x*)	Returns a string indicating the data type of *x*.

You can also *nest* functions — meaning that you can put functions inside functions. For example, when z = -999.9999, the expression print(int(abs(z))) prints the integer portion of the absolute value of z, which is 999. The original number is converted to positive, and then the decimal point and everything to its right are chopped off.

Still More Math Functions

In addition to the built-in functions covered so far, there are still others that you can import from the math module. If you need them in an app, put import math near the top of the .py file to make those functions available to the rest of the code. Or to use them at the command prompt, first enter the import math command.

One of the functions in the math module is the sqrt() function, which gets the square root of a number. Because it's part of the math module, you can't use it without importing the module first. For example, if you enter the following, you'll get an error because sqrt() isn't a built-in function:

```
print(sqrt(81))
```

Even if you do two commands like the following, you'll still get an error because you're treating sqrt() as a built-in function:

```
import math
print(sqrt(81))
```

To use a function from a module, you have to import the module *and* precede the function name with the module name and a dot. So let's say you have some value, x, and you want the square root. You have to import the math module and use math.sqrt(x) to get the correct answer, as shown in Figure 5-1. Entering that command shows 9.0 as the result, which is indeed the square root of 81.

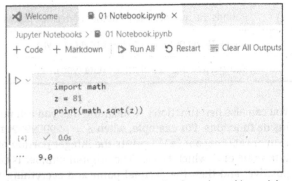

FIGURE 5-1: Using the sqrt() function from the math module.

The math module offers a lot of trigonometric and hyperbolic functions, powers and logarithms, angular conversions, and constants such as pi and e. We don't delve into all of them because advanced math isn't relevant to most people. You can check them all out anytime by searching the web for *python 3 math module functions*. Table 5-2 offers examples that may prove useful in your own work.

TABLE 5-2   Some Functions from the Python Math Module

Built-In Function	Purpose
math.acos(x)	Returns the arccosine of x in radians.
math.atan(x)	Returns the arctangent of x, in radians.
math.atan2(y, x)	Returns the arc tangent of y divided by x in radians.
math.ceil(x)	Returns the ceiling of x, the smallest integer greater than or equal to x.
math.cos(x)	Returns the cosine of x radians.
math.degrees(x)	Converts angle x from radians to degrees.
math.e	Returns the mathematical constant e (2.718281 . . .).
math.exp(x)	Returns e raised to the power x, where e is the base of natural logarithms.
math.factorial(x)	Returns the factorial of x.
math.floor(x)	Returns the floor of x, the largest integer less than or equal to x.
math.isnan(x)	Returns True if x is not a number; otherwise returns False. More specifically, this function returns True if x contains NaN, a special value in Python used as a placeholder for numeric variables that don't contain a number.
math.log(x, y)	Returns the logarithm of x to base y.
math.log2(x)	Returns the base-2 logarithm of x.
math.pi	Returns the mathematical constant pi (3.141593 . . .).
math.pow(x, y)	Returns x raised to the power y.

(continued)

TABLE 5-2 *(continued)*

Built-In Function	Purpose
math.radians(x)	Converts angle x from degrees to radians.
math.sin(x)	Returns the sine of x, (when x is expressed in radians).
math.sqrt(x)	Returns the square root of x.
math.tan(x)	Returns the tangent of x radians.
math.tau()	Returns the mathematical constant tau (6.283185 . . .).

Formatting Numbers

Over the years, Python has offered different methods for displaying numbers in formats familiar to us humans. For example, most people would rather see dollar amounts expressed in the format $1,234.56 than 1234.560065950695405695405959. The easiest way to format numbers in Python, starting with version 3.6, is to use f-stings.

Formatting with f-strings

Format strings, or *f-strings*, are the easiest way to format data in Python. All you need is a lowercase *f* or uppercase *F* followed immediately by some text or expressions enclosed in quotation marks. Here is an example:

```
f"Hello {username}"
```

The f before the first quotation mark tells Python that what follows is a format string. Inside the quotation marks, the text, called the *literal part*, is displayed literally (exactly as typed in the f-string). Anything in curly braces is the *expression part* of the f-string, a placeholder for what will appear when the code executes. Inside the curly braces, you can have an *expression* (a formula to perform some calculation, a variable name, or a combination of the two). Here is an example:

```
username = "Alan"
print(f"Hello {username}")
```

When you run this code, the print function displays the word Hello, followed by a space, followed by the contents of the username variable, as shown in Figure 5-2.

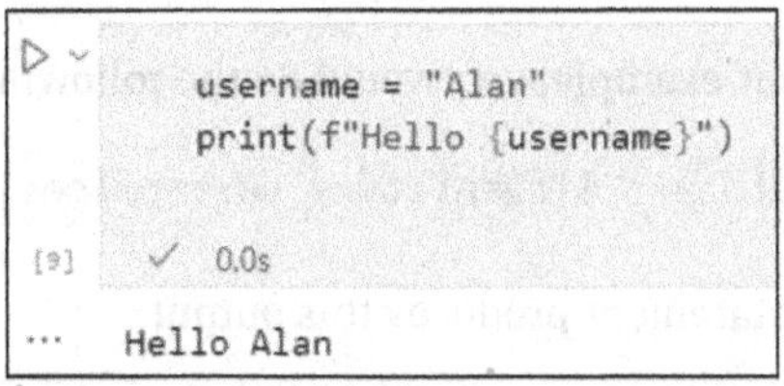

```
username = "Alan"
print(f"Hello {username}")

[9]   ✓ 0.0s

...   Hello Alan
```

FIGURE 5-2: A super simple f-string for formatting.

Here is another example of an expression — the formula quantity times unit_price — inside the curly braces:

```
unit_price = 49.99
quantity = 30
print(f"Subtotal: ${quantity * unit_price}")
```

The output from that, when executed, follows:

```
Subtotal: $1499.7
```

That $1499.7 isn't an ideal way to show dollar amounts. Typically, we like to use commas in the thousands places, and two digits for the pennies, as in the following:

```
Subtotal: $1,499.70
```

Fortunately, f-strings provide you with the means to do this formatting, as you learn next.

Showing dollar amounts

To get a comma to appear in the dollar amount and the pennies as two digits, you can use a *format string* inside the curly braces of an expression in an f-string. The format string starts with a colon and needs to be placed inside the closing curly brace, right up against the variable name or the value shown.

To show commas in thousands places, use a comma in your format string right after the colon, like this:

```
:,
```

Using the current example, you would do the following:

```
print(f"Subtotal: ${quantity * unit_price:,}")
```

Executing this statement produces this output:

```
Subtotal: $1,499.7
```

To get the pennies to show as two digits, follow the comma with

```
.2f
```

The .2f means "two decimal places, fixed" (never any more or less than two decimal places). The following code will display the number with commas and two decimal places:

```
print(f"Subtotal: ${quantity * unit_price:,.2f}")
```

Here's what the code displays when executed:

```
Subtotal: $1,499.70
```

Perfect! That's exactly the format we want. So anytime you want to show a number with commas in the thousands places and exactly two digits after the decimal point, use an f-string with the format string, .2f.

Formatting percent numbers

Now, suppose your app applies sales tax. The app needs to know the sales tax rate, which should be expressed as a decimal number. So if the sales tax rate is 6.5 percent, it has to be written as 0.065 (or .065, if you prefer) in your code, like this:

```
sales_tax_rate = 0.065
```

It's the same amount with or without the leading zero, so just use whichever format works for you.

This number format is ideal for Python, and you wouldn't want to mess with that. But if you want to display that number to a human, simply using a print() function displays it exactly as Python stores it:

```
sales_tax_rate = 0.065
print(f"Sales Tax Rate {sales_tax_rate}")
Sales Tax Rate 0.065
```

When displaying the sales tax rate for people to read, you'll probably want to use the more familiar 6.5% format rather than .065. You can use the same idea as with fixed numbers (.2f). However, you replace the f for fixed numbers with %, like this:

```
print(f"Sales Tax Rate {sales_tax_rate:.2%}")
```

Running this code multiples the sales tax rate by 100 and follows it with a percent sign (%).

Formatting width and alignment

You can also control the width of your output (and the alignment of content within that width) by following the colon in your f-string with < (for left aligned), ^ (for centered), or > (for right aligned). Put any of these characters right after the colon in your format string. For example, the following will make the output 20 characters wide, with the content right aligned:

```
:>20
```

TIP

Anytime you need a reminder about the complicated print f stuff, just ask ChatGPT or other generative AI for a reminder. For example, you can ask it to *write python print f for right-aligned currency numbers with two decimal places* or *write a python print f for two-digit percentage values*. Then copy and paste whatever AI produces into your own code, and adjust it to your current needs.

Grappling with Weirder Numbers

Most of us deal with simple numbers like quantities and dollar amounts all the time. If your work requires you to deal with bases other than 10 or imaginary numbers, Python has the stuff you need to do the job. But keep in mind that you don't need to learn these things to use Python or any other language. You would use these only if your actual work (or perhaps homework) requires it. In the next section, you look at some number types commonly used in computer science: binary, octal, and hexadecimal numbers.

If your work requires dealing with base 2, base 8, or base 16 numbers, you're in luck because Python has symbols for writing these as well as functions for converting among them. Table 5-3 shows the three non-decimal bases and the digits used by each.

TABLE 5-3 **Python for Base 2, 8, and 16 Numbers**

System	Also Called	Digits Used	Symbol	Function
Base 2	Binary	0, 1	0b	bin( )
Base 8	Octal	0, 1, 2, 3, 4, 5, 6, 7	0b	oct( )
Base 16	Hexadecimal or hex	0, 1, 2, 3, 4, 5, 6, 7, 8, 9, A, B, C, D, E, F	0x	hex( )

Most people never have to work with binary, octal, or hexadecimal numbers, so if all of this is giving you the heebie-jeebies, don't sweat it. If you've never heard of them before, chances are you'll never hear of them again after you've completed this section.

TIP

If you want more information about the various numbering systems, you can use your favorite search engine to search for *binary number* or *octal, decimal,* or *hexadecimal*.

Manipulating Strings

In Python and other programming languages, we refer to words and chunks of text as *strings,* short for "a string of characters." A string has no numeric meaning or value. (We discuss the basics of strings in Book 1, Chapter 4.) In this section, you learn Python coding skills for working with strings.

Concatenating strings

You can join strings by using a plus sign (+). The process of doing so is called *string concatenation* in nerd-o-rama world. One thing that catches beginners off guard is the fact that a computer doesn't know a word from a bologna sandwich. So when you join strings, the computer doesn't automatically put spaces where you'd expect them. For example, in the following code, full_name is a concatenation of the first three strings.

```python
first_name = "Alan"
middle_init = "C"
last_name = "Simpson"
full_name = first_name + middle_init + last_name
print(full_name)
```

When you run this code to print the contents of the full_name variable, you can see that Python did join them in one long string:

```
AlanCSimpson
```

Nothing is wrong with this output, per se, except that we usually put spaces between words and the parts of a person's name.

Because Python won't automatically put in spaces where you think they should go, you have to put them in yourself. The easiest way to represent a single space is by using a pair of quotation marks with one space between them, like this:

```
" "
```

If you forget to put the space between the quotation marks, like the following, you won't get a space in your string because there's no space between the quotation marks:

```
""
```

You can put multiple spaces between the quotation marks if you want multiple spaces in your output, but typically one space is enough. In the following example, you put a space between first_name and last_name. You also stick a period and space after middle_init:

```python
first_name = "Alan"
middle_init = "C"
last_name = "Simpson"
```

```
full_name = first_name + " " + middle_init + ". "
    + last_name
print(full_name)
```

The output of this code, which is the contents of that `full_name` variable, looks more like the kind of name you're used to seeing:

```
Alan C. Simpson
```

Of course, as an alternative to concatenating all the components and spaces together in a new string, you can simply display the name in the desired format using an f-string, as in the following code. The only difference is that you don't have a variable named `full_name` to work with in your code.

```
print(f"{first_name} {middle_init}. {last_name}")
```

Getting the length of a string

To determine how many characters are in a string, you use the built-in `len()` function (short for *length*). The length includes spaces because spaces are characters, each one having a length of one. An empty string — that is, a string with nothing in it, not even a space — has a length of zero.

Working with common string operators

Python offers several operators for working with sequences of data. One weird thing about strings in Python (and in most other programming languages) is that when you're counting characters, the first character counts as 0, not 1. This makes no sense to us humans, but computers count characters that way because it's the most efficient method. So even though the string is five characters long, the last character in that string is the letter *E*, because the first character is number 0. Go figure.

Table 5-4 summarizes the Python 3 operators for working with strings.

TABLE 5-4 **Python Sequence Operators That Work with Strings**

Operator	Purpose
x in *s*	Returns True if the string *x* exists somewhere in string *s*.
x not in *s*	Returns True if *x* is not contained in string *s*.
s * *n* or *n* * *s*	Repeats string *s* *n* times.
s[*i*]	The character at position *i* within string *s*.
s[*i*:*j*]	A slice from string *x* beginning with the character at position *i* up to (but excluding) the character at position *j*.
s[*i*:*j*:*k*]	A slice of *s* from *i* to *j* with step *k* where *k* is the distance between any characters. For example, setting *k* to 2 displays every other character. Setting *k* to 3 returns every third character, and so forth.
min(s)	The smallest (lowest) character of string *s*.
max(s)	The largest (highest) character of string *s*.

When the output of a `print()` function doesn't look right, keep in mind two important facts about strings in Python:

>> The first character is always number 0.

>> Every space counts as one character, so don't skip spaces when counting.

You may have noticed that `min(s)` returns a blank space, meaning that the blank space character is the lowest character in that string. But what exactly makes the space "lower" than the letter *A* or the letter *a*? The simple answer is the letter's *ASCII number*. Every character you can type at your keyboard, and many additional characters, have a number assigned by the American Standard Code for Information Interchange (ASCII).

Manipulating strings with methods

Every string in Python 3 is considered a *str object* (pronounced "string object"). The shortened word *str* for *string* distinguishes Python 3 from earlier versions of Python, which referred to strings as string objects (with the word *string* spelled out, not shortened). This naming convention is a great source of confusion, especially for beginners. Just try to remember that in Python 3, str is all about strings of characters.

Python offers numerous *str methods* (also called *string methods*) to help you work with str objects. The general syntax of str object methods is as follows:

```
string.methodname(params)
```

where `string` is the string you're analyzing, `methodname` is the name of a method from Table 5-5, and `params` refers to any parameters that you need to pass to the method (if required). The leading s in the first column of Table 5-5 means "any string," be it a literal string enclosed in quotation marks or the name of a variable that contains a string.

TABLE 5-5   Built-In Methods for Python 3 Strings

Method	Purpose
s.capitalize()	Returns a string with the first letter capitalized and the rest lowercase.
s.count(x, [y, z])	Returns the number of times string x appears in string s. Optionally, you can add y as a starting point and z as an ending point to search a portion of the string.
s.find(x, [y, z])	Returns a number indicating the first position at which string x can be found in string s. Optional y and z parameters allow you to limit the search to a portion of the string. Returns −1 if none found.
s.index(x, [y, z])	Similar to find but raises a "substring not found" error if string x can't be found in string y.
s.isalpha()	Returns True if s is at least one character long and contains only letters (A–Z or a–z) and printable Unicode characters.
s.isdecimal()	Returns True if s is at least one character long and contains only numeric characters (0–9).
s.islower()	Returns True if s contains letters and all those letters are lowercase.

Method	Purpose
s.isnumeric()	Returns True if s is at least one character long and contains only numeric characters (0–9).
s.isprintable()	Returns True if string s contains only printable characters. Spaces are considered printable, but newlines and tabs are not.
s.istitle()	Returns True if string s contains letters and the first letter of each word is uppercase followed by lowercase letters.
s.isupper()	Returns True if all letters in the string are uppercase.
s.lower()	Returns s with all letters converted to lowercase.
s.lstrip()	Returns s with any leading whitespace (spaces, tabs, newlines) removed.
s.replace(x, y)	Returns a copy of string s with string x replaced by string y.
s.rfind(x, [y, z])	Similar to s.find but searches backward from the start of the string. If y and z are provided, searches backward from position z to position y. Returns –1 if string x not found.
s.rindex()	Same as s.rfind but raises an error if the substring isn't found.
s.rstrip()	Returns string s with any trailing whitespace removed.
s.strip()	Returns string s with leading and trailing whitespace removed.
s.swapcase()	Returns string s with uppercase letters converted to lowercase and lowercase letters converted to uppercase.
s.title()	Returns string s with the first letter of every word capitalized and all other letters lowercase.
s.upper()	Returns string s with all letters converted to uppercase.

Don't bother trying to memorize or even make sense of every string method. Remember, you can always ask generative AI to list all the string operators and functions for you. Or search the web for *python string methods* to find out what's available.

Uncovering Dates and Times

In the world of computers, we often use dates and times for scheduling, or for calculating when something is due or how many days it's past due. We sometimes use *timestamps* to record exactly when a user did something or when an event occurred. There are lots of reasons for using dates and times in Python, but perhaps surprisingly, no built-in data type for them exists like the ones for strings and numbers.

To work with dates and times, you typically need to use the `datetime` module. As with any module, you must import it before you can use it. You do that using `import datetime`. And as with any import, you can add an alias (nickname) that's easier to type, if you like. For example, `import datetime as dt` would work, too. You just have to remember to type `dt` rather than `datetime` in your code when calling upon the capabilities of that module.

The `datetime` module provides an easy way to work with dates and times in Python. It provides three ways of storing information about dates, times, and time zones including these:

>> `datetime.date`: A date consisting of month, day, and year (but no time information).

>> `datetime.time`: A time consisting of hour, minute, second, microsecond, and optionally time zone information if needed (but no date).

>> `datetime.datetime`: A single item of data consisting of date, time, and, optionally, time zone information.

We preceded each type with the full word `datetime` in the preceding list, but if you use an alias, such as `dt`, you can use that in your code instead. We talk about each of these data types separately in the sections that follow.

Working with dates

The `datetime.date` data type is ideal for working with dates when time isn't an issue. You can create a date object in two ways. You can get today's date from the computer's internal clock by using the today() method. Or you can specify a year, month, and day (in that order) inside parentheses.

When specifying the month or day, never use a leading zero for datetime.date(). For example, April 1 2024 has to be expressed as 2024,4,1 — if you type 2024,04,01, it won't work.

After importing the datetime module, you can use date.today() to get the current date from the computer's internal clock. Or use date(*year, month, day*) syntax to create a date object for some other date. The following code shows both methods:

```
# Import the datetime module, nickname dt
import datetime as dt
# Store today's date in a variable named today.
today = dt.date.today()
# Store some other date in a variable called
    last_of_teens
last_of_teens = dt.date(2019, 12, 31)
```

You can isolate any part of a date object by using .month, .day, or .year. For example, in the same Python prompt, execute this code:

```
print(last_of_teens.month)
print(last_of_teens.day)
print(last_of_teens.year)
```

Each of the three components of that date appear on a separate line:

```
12
31
2023
```

You can format dates and times however you want. Use f-strings, which we discuss earlier in this chapter, along with the string formatting directives shown on https://docs.python.org/3/library/datetime.html about three-quarters of the way down from the top of the page, which includes the format for dates as well as for times, as we discuss later in this chapter. For directives that show local dates and time, the exact format will depend on your location. For example, using %x to display the date December 18, 2023 in the U.S. would show 12/18/23 but 18/12/2023 in countries where it's more common to show the day first, rather than the month.

When using format strings, make sure you put spaces, slashes, and anything else you want between directives where you want those to appear in the output. For example, this line:

```
print(f"{last_of_teens:%A, %B %d, %Y}")
```

when executed, displays this:

```
Tuesday, December 31, 2019
```

To show the date in the *mm/dd/yyyy* format, use %m/%d/%Y, like this:

```
todays_date = f"{today:%m/%d/%Y}"
```

The output will be the current date for you when you try it, with a format like the following:

```
11/19/2024
```

Table 5-6 shows a few more examples you can try with different dates.

TABLE 5-6 **Sample Date Format Strings**

Format String	Example
%a, %b %d %Y	Sat, Jun 01 2024
%x	06/01/24
%m-%d-%y	06-01-24
This %A %B %d	This Saturday June 01
%A %B %d is day number %j of %Y	Saturday June 01 is day number 152 of 2024

Sometimes you want to work only with dates, and sometimes you want to work only with times. Often you want to pinpoint a moment in time using both the date and the time. For that, use the datetime class of the datetime module. This class supports a now() method that can grab the current date and time from the computer clock, as follows:

```
import datetime as dt
right_now = dt.datetime.now()
print(right_now)
```

What you see on the screen from the print() function depends on when you execute this code. But the format of the datetime value will be like this:

```
2024-11-19 14:03:07.525975
```

This means November 19, 2024 at 2:03 PM (with 7.525975 seconds tacked on).

You can also define a datetime using any the following parameters. The month, day, and year are required. The rest are optional and set to 0 in the time if you omit them.

```
datetime(year, month, day, hour, [minute, [second,
    [microsecond]]])
```

Here is an example using 11:59 PM on December 31 2024:

```
import datetime as dt
new_years_eve = dt.datetime(2024, 12, 31, 23, 59)
print(new_years_eve)
```

Here is the output of that print() statement with no formatting:

```
2024-12-31 23:59:00
```

Table 5-7 shows examples of formatting the datetime.

TABLE 5-7 **Sample Datetime Format Strings**

Format String	Example
%A, %B %d at %I:%M%p	Tuesday, December 31 at 11:59PM
%m/%d/%y at %H:%M%p	12/31/24 at 23:59PM
%I:%M %p on %b %d	11:59 PM on Dec 31
%x	12/31/24
%c	Tue Dec 31 23:59:00 2024
%m/%d/%y at %I:%M %p	12/31/24 at 11:59 PM
%I:%M %p on %m/%d/%y	1:59 PM on 12/31/2024

Calculating timespans

Sometimes just knowing the date or time isn't enough. You need to know the duration, or *timespan*, as it's typically called in the computer world. In other words, not the date, not the o'clock, but the "how long" in terms of years, months, weeks, days, hours, minutes, or whatever. For timespans, the Python datetime module includes the datetime.timedelta class.

A timedelta object is created automatically whenever you subtract two dates, times, or datetimes to determine the duration between them. For example, suppose you create a couple of variables to store dates, perhaps one for New Year's Day and another for Memorial Day. Then you create a third variable named days_between and put in it the difference you get by subtracting the earlier date from the later date, as follows:

```python
import datetime as dt
new_years_day = dt.date(2024, 1, 1)
memorial_day = dt.date(2024, 5, 27)
days_between = memorial_day - new_years_day
print(days_between)
print(type(days_between))
```

So what exactly is days_between in terms of a data type? If you print its value, you get 147 days, 0:00:00. In other words, there are 147 days between those dates; the 0:00:00 is time, but because we didn't specify a time of day in either date, the time digits are all just set to 0. If you use the Python type() function to determine the data type of days_between, you see that it's a timedelta object from the datetime class, as follows:

```
147 days, 0:00:00
<class 'datetime.timedelta'>
```

The timedelta calculation happens automatically when you subtract one date from another to get the time between. You can also define any timedelta (duration) using this syntax:

```
datetime.timedelta(days=, seconds=, microseconds=,
    milliseconds=, minutes=, hours=, weeks=)
```

TIP

Generative AI can write complicated date/time code for you, too. For example, you can ask Copilot in VS Code, ChatGPT, or other services to "write Python code to calculate the time between two dates" or "write Python code to display the current date and time in U.S. format."

Chapter **6**
Controlling the Action

So far in this book we've talked a lot about storing information in computers, mostly in variables that Python and your computer can work with. Having the information in a form that the computer can work with is critical to getting a computer to do anything. Think of this as the "having" part — having some information with which to work.

But now we need to turn our attention to the "doing" part — working with that information to create something useful or entertaining. In this chapter, we cover the most important and most commonly used operations for making the computer *do* stuff. We start with something that computers do well, do quickly, and do a lot: make decisions.

Main Operators for Controlling the Action

You control what your program (and the computer) does by making decisions, which often involves making comparisons. You use operators, such as those in Table 6-1, to make comparisons. These operators are often referred to as *relational operators* or *comparison operators* because by comparing items, the computer is determining how two items are related.

TABLE 6-1 **Python Comparison Operators for Decision-Making**

Operator	Meaning
==	Is equal to
!=	Is not equal to
<	Is less than
>	Is greater than
<=	Is less than or equal to
>=	Is greater than or equal to

Python also offers three *logical operators*, also called *Boolean operators*, which enable you assess multiple comparisons before making a final decision. These operators use the English word for, well, basically what they mean, as shown in Table 6-2.

TABLE 6-2 **Python Logical Operators**

Operator	Meaning
and	Both are true
or	One or the other is true
not	Is not true

All these operators are often used with if ... then ... else decisions to control what an app or program does. To make such decisions, you use the Python if statement.

Making Decisions with if

The word *if* is used a lot in all apps and computer programs to make decisions. The simplest syntax for *if* follows:

```
if condition: do this
do this no matter what
```

So the first do this line is executed only if the condition is true. If the condition is false, that first do this is ignored. Regardless of what the condition turns out to be, the second line is executed next. Note that neither line is indented. Indentation means a lot in Python, as you'll see shortly. But first, consider a few simple examples with this simple syntax. You can try it for yourself in a .py file.

Figure 6-1 shows a simple example in which the sun variable receives the down string. Then an if statement checks to see whether the sun variable equals the word down and, if it does, prints a Good night! message. Then it just continues on normally to print an I am here message.

```
sun = "down"
if sun == "down": print("Good night!")
print("I am here")

    Good night!
    I am here
```

FIGURE 6-1: The result of a simple if when the condition proves true.

WARNING

Make sure you always use two equal signs with no space between (==) to test equality. This rule is easy to forget. If you type it incorrectly, the code won't work as expected.

REMEMBER

You must spell True and False with an initial capital letter and the rest lowercase. If you type it any other way, Python won't recognize it as a Boolean True or False and your code won't run as expected.

Notice that in the if statement, we used

```
if taxable:
```

This code is perfectly okay because we made taxable a Boolean that can only be True or False. You may see other people type it as

```
if taxable == True:
```

Adding else to your if logic

So far, you've looked at code examples in which some code is executed if some condition proves true. If the condition proves false, that code is ignored. Sometimes, you may want one chunk of code to execute *if* a condition proves true; *otherwise* (*else*), if it doesn't prove true, you want some other chunk of code to be executed. In that case, you can add an `else:` to your `if`. Any lines of code indented under the `else:` are executed only if the condition did not prove true. Here is the logic and syntax:

```
if condition:
    do indented lines here
    ...
else:
    do indented lines here
    ...
do remaining un-indented lines no matter what
```

Figure 6-2 shows a simple example in which we grab the current time from the computer clock using `datetime.now()`. If the hour of that time is less than 12, the program displays Good morning. Otherwise, it displays Good afternoon. Regardless of the hour, it prints I hope you are doing well! So if you write such a program and run it in the morning, you get the appropriate greeting followed by I hope you are doing well!, as in Figure 6-2.

```
import datetime as dt
# Get the current date and time
now = dt.datetime.now()
# Make a decision based on hour
if now.hour < 12:
    print("Good morning")
else:
    print("Good afternoon")
print("I hope you are doing well!")

    Good morning
    I hope you are doing well!
```

FIGURE 6-2: Print an initial greeting based on the time of day.

When `if ... else` isn't enough to handle all the possibilities, there's `elif` (which, as you may have guessed, is a word made up from `else if`). An `if` statement can include any number of `elif` conditions. You can include or not include a final `else` statement that executes only if the `if` and all the previous `elif`s prove false.

In its simplest form, the syntax for an `if` with `elif` without an `else` statement is

```
if condition:
    do these indented lines of code
    ...
elif condition:
    do these indented lines of code
    ...
do these un-indented lines of code no matter what
```

Comments are always optional. But adding comments to the code can make it easier to understand, for future reference:

```
age = 31
if age < 21:
    # If under 21, no alcohol
    beverage = "milk"
elif age >= 21 and age < 80:
    # Ages 21 - 79, suggest beer
    beverage = "beer"
else:
    # If 80 or older, prune juice might be a good
  choice.
    beverage = "prune juice"
print("Have a " + beverage)
```

REMEMBER

If you forget all the syntax rules for `if ... elif ... else`, you can just ask Copilot, ChatGPT, Claude.ai, or another generative AI to *write a python if elif else statement* for you. You should get some generic code with the right syntax to get you started.

Ternary operations

`If ... then ... else` operations are very common, and many programming languages offer a shorthand syntax for creating them. They're usually called *ternary* operators but the Python documentation often refers to them as *conditional expressions*. They serve exactly the same purpose as `if ... else`. So there is nothing new being added here. It's just an alternative syntax with few words. The basic blueprint is

```
value_if_true if condition else value_if_false
```

As a working example, take a look at the following code:

```
# Sales tax rate value depends on taxable status
sales_tax_rate = 0.065 if taxable else 0
```

Repeating a Process with for

Decision-making is a big part of writing all kinds of apps — games, artificial intelligence, robotics . . . whatever. But sometimes you need to count or perform a task over and over. For those times, you can use a *for loop*, which enables you to repeat a line of code, or several lines of code, as many times as you like.

Looping through numbers in a range

If you know how many times you want a loop to repeat, using the following syntax may be easiest:

```
for x in range(y):
    do this
    do this
    . . .
un-indented code is executed after the loop
```

Replace *x* with any variable name of your choosing. Replace *y* with any number or range of numbers. If you specify one number, the range will be from 0 to 1 less than the final number. For example, run this code in a .py file:

```
for x in range(7):
    print(x)
print("All done")
```

The output is the result of executing print(x) once for each pass through the loop, with x starting at 0. The final line, which isn't indented, executes after the loop has finished looping. So the output is

```
0
1
```

```
2
3
4
5
6
All done
```

You might have expected the loop to count from 1 to 7 instead of 0 to 6. However, unless you specify otherwise, the loop always starts counting from 0. If you want to start counting with another number, specify the starting number and the ending number, separated by a comma, inside the parentheses. When you specify two numbers, the first number identifies where the counting starts. The second number is 1 greater than where the loop stops (which is unfortunate for readability, but such is life).

Looping through a list

In Python, a *list* is basically any group of items, separated by commas, inside square brackets. You can loop through such a list using a for loop. In the following example, the list to loop through is specified in brackets on the first line:

```python
for x in ["The", "rain", "in", "Spain"]:
    print(x)
print("Done")
```

This kind of loop repeats once for each item in the list. The x variable gets its value from one item in the list, going from left to right. So, running the preceding code produces the output you see in Figure 6-3.

FIGURE 6-3: Looping through a list.

Bailing out of a loop

Typically, you want a loop to go through an entire list or range of items, but you can also force a loop to stop early if some condition is met. Use the break statement inside an if statement to force the loop to stop early. The syntax is

```
for x in items:
if condition:
    [do this ... ]
    break
do this
```

The square brackets in this example aren't part of the code. They indicate that what is between the brackets is optional. Suppose that someone completed an exam and we want to loop through the answers. But we have a rule that says if an answer is empty, we mark it Incomplete and ignore the rest of the items in the list. In the following, all items are answered (no blanks):

```
answers = ["A", "C", "B", "D"]
for answer in answers:
    if answer == "":
        print("Incomplete")
        break
    print(answer)
print("Loop is done")
```

In the result, all four answers are printed:

```
A
C
B
D
Loop is done
```

So the logic is, as long as some answer is provided, the if code is not executed and the loop runs to completion. However, if the loop encounters a blank answer, it prints Incomplete and also "breaks" the loop, jumping down to the first statement outside the loop (the final un-indented statement), which prints Loop is done.

Looping with continue

You can also use a `continue` statement in a loop, which is kind of the opposite of `break`. Whereas `break` makes code execution jump past the end of the loop and stop looping, `continue` makes it jump back to the top of the loop and continue with the next item (that is, after the item that triggered the `continue`). So here is the same code as the preceding example, but instead of executing a `break` when execution hits a blank answer, it continues with the next item in the list:

```
answers = ["A", "C", "", "D"]
for answer in answers:
    if answer == "":
        print("Incomplete")
        continue
    print(answer)
print("Loop is done")
```

The output of that code is as follows. It doesn't print the blank answer, it prints `Incomplete`, but then it goes back and continues looping through the rest of the items:

```
A
C
Incomplete
D
Loop is done
```

Nesting loops

It's perfectly okay to *nest* loops — that is, to put loops inside loops. Just make sure you get your indentations right because the indentations determine which loop, if any, a line of code is located within. For example, in Figure 6-4, an outer loop loops through the words `First`, `Second`, and `Third`. With each pass through the loop, it prints a word and then it prints the numbers 1–3 (by looping through a range and adding 1 to each range value).

The loops work because each word in the outer list is followed by the numbers 1–3. The end of the loop is the first un-indented line at the bottom, which doesn't print until the outer loop has completed its process.

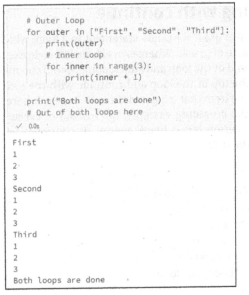

```
# Outer Loop
for outer in ["First", "Second", "Third"]:
    print(outer)
    # Inner Loop
    for inner in range(3):
        print(inner + 1)

print("Both loops are done")
# Out of both loops here
```
✓ 0.0s

```
First
1
2
3
Second
1
2
3
Third
1
2
3
Both loops are done
```

FIGURE 6-4: Nested loops.

Looping with while

As an alternative to looping with for, you can loop with while. The difference is subtle. With for, you generally get a fixed number of loops, one for each item in a range or one for each item in a list. With a while loop, the loop keeps going *as long as* (while) some condition is true. Here is the basic syntax:

```
while condition:
    do this ...
    do this ...
do this when the loop is done
```

With while loops, you have to make sure that the *condition* that makes the loop stop happens eventually. Otherwise, you get an infinite loop that just keeps going and going and going until some error causes it to fail, or until you force it to stop by closing the app, shutting down the computer, or doing some other awkward thing.

The easy and common mistake to make with this kind of loop is to forget to increment the counter so that it grows with each pass through the loop and eventually makes the `while` condition `False` and stops the loop. In Figure 6-5, we intentionally removed `counter += 1` to cause that error. As you can see, the loop keeps printing A. It keeps going until you stop it, or it runs out of memory and stops on its own.

```
ℂ jupyter  If Decisions  Last Checkpoint: 5 hours ago  (unsaved changes)

File   Edit   View   Insert   Cell   Kernel   Widgets   Help

⊞  +  ✂  🗅  📋  ↑  ↓  ▶ Run  ■  ℂ  ▶▶  Code          ▼  ▦
                              │ Interrupt the kernel │

In [*]:  counter = 65
         while counter < 91:
             print(str(counter) + "=" + chr(counter))
         print("all done")
         65=A
         65=A
         65=A
         65=A
         65=A
         65=A
         65=A
         65=A
         65=A
         65=A
         65=A
         65=A
         65=A
         65=A
         65=A
         65=A
         65=A
         65=A
         65=A
```

FIGURE 6-5: An infinite `while` loop.

TIP

If you forget the syntax for writing a Python loop and want a quick example, just ask Copilot or other generative AI to *write a python for loop* or *write a python while loop* or *write a python loop that repeats for each character in a string*. Say whatever words best describe the code you're trying to write at the moment.

Starting while loops over with continue

You can use `if` and `continue` in a `while` loop to skip back to the top of the loop just as you can with `for` loops. Take a look at the code in Figure 6-6 for an example.

A `while` loop keeps going while a variable named `counter` is less than 10. Inside the loop, the variable named `number` is assigned a random number in the range of 1 to 999. Then the following statement checks to see whether `number` is even:

```
if int(number / 2) == number / 2:
```

```
import random
print("Odd numbers")
counter = 0
while counter < 10:
    # Get a random number
    number = random.randint(1,999)
    if int(number / 2) == number /2:
        # If it's an even number, don't print it.
        continue
    #Otherwise, if it's odd, print it and increment the couter.
    print(number)
    # Increment the loop counter.
    counter += 1
print("Loop is done")
```

```
Odd numbers
697
449
91
567
949
333
591
699
895
837
Loop is done
```

FIGURE 6-6: A while loop with continue.

Breaking while loops with break

You can also break a while loop using break, just as you can with a for loop. When you break a while loop, you force execution to continue with the first line of code under and outside the loop, thereby stopping the loop but continuing the flow with the rest of the action after the loop.

Chapter **7**

Speeding Along with Lists and Tuples

S ometimes in code you work with one item of data at a time, such as a person's name or a unit price or a username. Other times, you work with larger sets of data, such as a list of people's names or a list of products and their prices. These sets of data are often referred to as *lists* or *arrays* in most programming languages.

Python has lots of easy, fast, and efficient ways to deal with all kinds of data collections, as you discover in this chapter. As always, we encourage you to follow along in a .py file. The "doing" part helps with the "understanding" part.

Defining and Using Lists

The simplest data collection in Python is a list. We provided examples of these in the preceding chapter. A *list* is any list of data items, separated by commas, inside square brackets. Typically, you assign a name to the list using an = character, just as you would with variables. If the list contains numbers, don't use quotation marks around them. For example, here is a list of test scores:

```
scores = [88, 92, 78, 90, 98, 84]
```

If the list contains strings, those strings should, as always, be enclosed in single or double quotation marks, as in this example:

```
students = ["Mark", "Amber", "Todd", "Anita",
    "Sandy"]
```

To display the contents of a list on the screen, you can print it just as you would print any regular variable. For example, executing `print(students)` in your code after defining that list displays the following on the screen:

```
['Mark', 'Amber', 'Todd', 'Anita', 'Sandy']
```

This output may not be exactly what you had in mind. But don't worry: Python offers lots of ways to display lists.

Referencing list items by position

Each item in a list has a position number, starting with 0, even though you don't see any numbers. You can refer to any item in the list by its number using the name for the list followed by a number in square brackets. In other words, use this syntax:

```
listname[x]
```

Replace *listname* with the name of the list you're accessing and replace *x* with the position number of the item you want. Remember, the first item is always 0, not 1. For example, in the following first line, we define a list named `students`, and then print item number 0 from that list. The result, when executing the code, is the name `Mark` displayed:

```
students = ["Mark", "Amber", "Todd", "Anita",
    "Sandy"]
print(students[0])
```

The next example shows a list named `scores`. The `print()` function prints the value of `scores[4]`, which is 84 in this example.

Remember, the first item is always at position 0. So scores[0] is 88, scores[1] is 92 and so forth.

```
scores = [88, 92, 78, 90, 84]
print(scores[4])
84
```

If you try to access a list item that doesn't exist, you get a list index out of range error. The *index* part is a reference to the number inside the square brackets.

Looping through a list

To access each item in a list, just use a for loop with this syntax:

```
for x in list:
```

Replace *x* with a variable name of your choosing. Replace *list* with the name of the list.

Seeing whether a list contains an item

If you want your code to check the contents of a list to see whether it already contains some item, use in *listname* in an if statement or a variable assignment. For example, the code in Figure 7-1 creates a list of names. Then, two variables store the results of searching the list for the names Anita and Bob. Printing the contents of each variable displays True for the one where the name Anita is in the list. The test to see whether Bob is in the list proves False.

```
students = ["Mark", "Amber", "Todd", "Anita", "Sandy"]

# Is Anita in the list?
has_anita = "Anita" in students
print(has_anita)

#Is Bob in the list?
has_bob = "Bob" in students
print(has_bob)

    True
    False
```

FIGURE 7-1: Seeing whether an item is in a list.

Getting the length of a list

To determine how many items are in a list, use the len() function (short for *length*). Put the name of the list inside the parentheses. For example, type the following code at the Python prompt:

```
students = ["Mark", "Amber", "Todd", "Anita",
    "Sandy"]
print(len(students))
```

Running that code produces this output:

```
5
```

The list has five items, though the index of the last item is always 1 less than the list's length, because Python starts counting at 0. So the last item, Sandy, is stored in students[4] and not students[5].

Adding an item to the end of a list

When you want your code to add an item to the end of a list, use the .append() method with the value you want to add inside the parentheses. You can use either a variable name or a literal value.

Inserting an item into a list

Whereas the append() method adds an item to the end of a list, the insert() method adds an item to the list in any position. The syntax for insert() is

```
listname.insert(position, item)
```

Changing an item in a list

You can change an item in a list using the = assignment operator just like you do with variables. Make sure you include the index number in square brackets to indicate which item you want to change. The syntax is

```
listname[index] = newvalue
```

Combining lists

If you have two lists that you want to combine into a single list, use the extend() function with the following syntax:

```
original_list.extend(additional_items_list)
```

In your code, replace *original_list* with the name of the list to which you'll be adding new list items. Replace *additional_items_list* with the name of the list that contains the items you want to add to the first list. Here is a simple example using lists named list1 and list2. After executing list1.extend(list2), the first list contains the items from both lists, as you can see in the output of the print() statement at the end.

```
# Create two lists of Names.
list1 = ["Zara", "Lupe", "Hong", "Alberto",
    "Jake"]
list2 = ["Huey", "Dewey", "Louie", "Nader",
    "Bubba"]
# Add list2 names to list1.
list1.extend(list2)
# Print list 1.
print(list1)

['Zara', 'Lupe', 'Hong', 'Alberto', 'Jake',
    'Huey', 'Dewey', 'Louie', 'Nader', 'Bubba']
```

Easy Parcheesi, no?

You can also join lists just by concatenating them with a plus sign (+). For example, you could use the line newlist = list1 + list2 to create a new list named newlist that contains all the items from both lists.

Removing list items

Python offers a remove() method so that you can remove any value from the list. If the item is in the list multiple times, only the first occurrence is removed. For example, the following code displays a list of letters with the letter C repeated a few times.

Then the code uses `letters.remove("C")` to remove the letter C from the list:

```
# Create a list of strings.
letters = ["A", "B", "C", "D", "C", "E", "C"]
# Remove "C" from the list.
letters.remove("C")
# Show me the new list.
print(letters)
```

When you execute this code, you'll see that only the first letter C has been removed:

```
['A', 'B', 'D', 'C', 'E', 'C']
```

If you want to remove an item based on its position in the list, use pop() with an index number rather than remove() with a value. If you want to remove the last item from the list, use pop() without an index number. For example, the following code creates a list, removes the first item (0), and then removes the last item (pop() with nothing in the parentheses). Printing the list proves that those two items have been removed:

```
# Create a list of strings.
letters = ["A", "B", "C", "D", "E", "F", "G"]
# Remove the first item.
letters.pop(0)
# Remove the last item.
letters.pop()
# Show me the new list.
print(letters)
```

Running the code shows that popping the first and last items did, indeed, work:

```
['B', 'C', 'D', 'E', 'F']
```

When you pop() an item off the list, you can store a copy of that value in some variable.

Clearing out a list

If you want to delete the contents of a list but not the list itself, use .clear(). The list still exists, but it contains no items. In other words, it's an empty list.

Counting how many times an item appears in a list

You can use a list's count() method to count how many times an item appears in a list. As with other list methods, the syntax is simple:

```
listname.count(x)
```

Replace listname with the name of your list, and x with the value you're looking for (or the name of a variable that contains that value).

Finding a list item's index

Python offers an .index() method that returns a number indicating the position of an item in a list, based on the index number. The syntax is

```
listname.index(x)
```

As always, replace listname with the name of the list you want to search. Replace x what whatever you're looking for (either a literal or a variable name, as always). Of course, there's no guarantee that the item is in the list or is in the list only once. If the item isn't in the list, an error occurs. If the item is in the list multiple times, the index of only the first matching item is returned.

Figure 7-2 shows an example where the program crashes at the line f_index = grades.index(look_for) because there is no F in the list.

```
# Create a list of strings.
grades = ["C", "B", "A", "D", "C", "B", "C"]

# Find the index for "B"
b_index = grades.index("B")

#Find the index for F
look_for = "F"
f_index = grades.index(look_for)

# Show the results.
print("The first B is index " + str(b_index))
print("There first "+ look_for + " is at " + str(f_index))
```

```
ValueError                                 Traceback (most recent call last)
<ipython-input-38-ee447e55d5c6> in <module>()
      7 #Find the index for F
      8 look_for = "F"
----> 9 f_index = grades.index(look_for)
     10
     11 # Show the results.

ValueError: 'F' is not in list
```

FIGURE 7-2: Program fails when trying to find the index of a nonexistent list item.

An easy way to get around this problem is to use an if statement to see whether an item is in the list before you try to get its index number. If the item isn't in the list, display a message saying so. Otherwise, get the index number and show it in a message. That code follows:

```
# Create a list of strings.
grades = ["C", "B", "A", "D", "C", "B", "C"]
# Decide what to look for
look_for = "F"
# See if the item is in the list.
if look_for in grades:
    # If it's in the list, get and show the index.
    print(str(look_for) + " is at index " +
  str(grades.index(look_for)))
else:
    # If not in the list, don't even try for index
  number.
    print(str(look_for) + " isn't in the list.")
```

Alphabetizing and sorting lists

Python offers a sort() method for sorting lists. In its simplest form, it alphabetizes the items in the list (if they're strings). If the list contains numbers, they're sorted smallest to largest. For a simple sort like that, just use sort() with empty parentheses:

```
listname.sort()
```

Replace *listname* with the name of your list.

Then we appended one date at a time to the list using the dt.date(*year*,*month*,*day*) syntax.

Reversing a list

You can also reverse the order of items in a list using the .reverse method. This is not the same as sorting in reverse. When you sort in reverse, you still sort: Z–A for strings, largest to smallest for numbers, and latest to earliest for dates. When you reverse a list, you simply reverse the items in the list, no matter their order, without trying to sort them. In the following code, we reverse the order of the names in the list and then print the list.

```
# Create a list of strings.
Names = ["Zara", "Lupe", "Hong", "Alberto",
    "Jake"]
# Reverse the list.
Names.reverse()
# Print the list.
Print(names)

['Jake', 'Alberto', 'Hong', 'Lupe', 'Zara']
```

Copying a list

If you need to work with a copy of a list so as not to alter the original list, use the .copy() method. For example, the following code is similar to the preceding code, except that instead of reversing the order of the original list, we make a copy of the list and reverse that one. Printing the contents of each list shows how the first list is still in the original order, whereas the second one is reversed:

```
# Create a list of strings.
names = ["Zara", "Lupe", "Hong", "Alberto",
    "Jake"]
```

```
# Make a copy of the list.
backward_names = names.copy()
# Reverse the copy.
backward_names.reverse()
# Print the list.
print(names)
print(backward_names)

['Zara', 'Lupe', 'Hong', 'Alberto', 'Jake']
['Jake', 'Alberto', 'Hong', 'Lupe', 'Zara']
```

Table 7-1 summarizes the methods you've learned about so far in this chapter. As you will see in upcoming chapters, these methods work with other kinds of *iterables* (a fancy name that means any list or list-like thing that you can go through one at a time).

TABLE 7-1 **Methods for Working with Lists**

Method	What It Does
append()	Adds an item to the end of the list
clear()	Removes all items from the list, leaving it empty
copy()	Makes a copy of a list
count()	Counts how many times an element appears in a list
extend()	Appends the items from one list to the end of another list
index()	Returns the index number (position) of an element in a list
insert()	Inserts an item into the list at a specific position
pop()	Removes an element from the list, and provides a copy of that item that you can store in a variable
remove()	Removes one item from the list
reverse()	Reverses the order of items in the list
sort()	Sorts the list in ascending order
sort(reverse= True)	Sorts the list in descending order

What's a Tuple and Who Cares?

In addition to lists, Python supports a data structure known as a tuple. Some people pronounce that like "*two*-pull." Some people pronounce it to rhyme with *couple*. But it's not spelled *tupple* or *touple*, so our best guess is that it's pronounced "two-pull." (Heck, for all we know, there may not be only one correct way to pronounce it, but that doesn't stop people from arguing about it.)

Anyway, despite the oddball name, a *tuple* is just an immutable list (like that tells you a lot). In other words, a tuple is a list, but you can't change it after it's defined. It's like a constant.

The syntax for creating a tuple is the same as the syntax for creating a list, except you don't use square brackets. You have to use parentheses, like this:

```
prices = (29.95, 9.98, 4.95, 79.98, 2.95)
```

Most of the techniques and methods that you learned for using lists back in Table 7-1 *don't* work with tuples because they are used to modify something in a list, and a tuple can't be modified. However, you can get the length of a tuple using len, like this:

```
print(len(prices))
```

You can use .count() to see how many times an item appears in a tuple. For example:

```
print(prices.count(4.95))
```

You can use in to see whether a value exists in a tuple, as in the following sample code:

```
print(4.95 in prices)
```

This returns True if the tuple contains 4.95 or False if it doesn't.

If an item exists in the tuple, you can get its index number. You'll get an error, though, if the item doesn't exist in the tuple. You can use in first to see whether the item exists before checking for its index number, and then you can return some nonsense value such as –1 if it doesn't exist, as in this code:

```
look_for = 12345
if look_for in prices:
    position = prices.index(look_for)
else:
    position = -1
print(position)
```

You can loop through the items in a tuple and display them in any format you want by using format strings. For example, this code displays each item with a leading dollar sign and two digits for the pennies:

```
# Loop through and display each item in the tuple.
for price in prices:
    print(f"${price:.2f}")
```

The output from running this code with the sample tuple follows:

```
$29.95
$9.98
$4.95
$79.98
$2.95
```

You can't change the value of an item in a tuple using this kind of syntax:

```
prices[1] = 234.56
```

You'll get an error message that reads TypeError: 'tuple' object does not support item assignment. This message is telling you that you can't use the assignment operator, =, to change the value of an item in a tuple because a tuple is immutable, meaning its content cannot be changed.

Any method that alters, or even just copies, data in a list causes an error when you try it with a tuple. So the list methods .append(), .clear(), .copy(), .extend(), .insert(), .pop(), .remove(),

.reverse(), and .sort() would fail when working with tuples. In short, a tuple makes sense if you want to *show* data to users without giving them any means to *change* any of the information.

Working with Sets

Python also offers *sets* as a means of organizing data. One difference between a set and a list is that the items in a set have no specific order. Even though you may define the set with the items in a certain order, none of the items get index numbers to identify their position.

To define a set, use curly braces where you use square brackets for a list and parentheses for a tuple. For example, here's a set with some numbers in it:

```
sample_set = {1.98, 98.9, 74.95, 2.5, 1, 16.3}
```

Sets are similar to lists and tuples in a few ways. You can use len() to determine how many items are in a set. Use in to determine whether an item is in a set.

But you can't get an item in a set based on its index number. Nor can you change an item already in the set. You can't change the order of items in a set either. So you can't use .sort() to sort the set or .reverse() to reverse its order.

You can add a single new item to a set using .add(), as in the following example:

```
sample_set.add(11.23)
```

Note that unlike a list, a set never contains more than one instance of a value. So even if you add 11.23 to the set multiple times, the set will still contain only one copy of 11.23.

You can also add multiple items to a set using .update(). But the items you're adding should be defined as a list in square brackets, as in the following example:

```
sample_set.update([88, 123.45, 2.98])
```

You can copy a set. However, because the set has no defined order, when you display the copy, its items may not be in the same order as the original set.

Lists and tuples are two of the most commonly used Python data structures. Sets don't seem to get as much play as the other two, but it's good to know about them.

Chapter **8**

Wrangling Bigger Chunks of Code

I n this chapter, you learn how to better manage larger code projects by creating your own functions. Functions provide a way to compartmentalize your code into small tasks that can be called from multiple places in an app. For example, if something you need to access throughout the app requires a dozen lines of code, chances are you don't want to repeat that code over and over every time you need it. Doing so just makes the code larger than it needs to be. Also, if you want to change something, or if you have to fix an error in that code, you don't want to have to do it repeatedly in a bunch of different places. If all that code were contained in a function, you would have to change or fix it in only one location.

To access the task that the function performs, you *call* the function from your code, just as you call a built-in function such as print. In other words, you just type the name into your code. You can make up your own function names, too. So, think of functions as a way to personalize the Python language so that its commands fit what you need in your application.

Creating a Function

Creating a function is easy. Follow along in a .py file if you want to get some hands-on experience.

To create a function, start a new line with def (short for *definition*) followed by a space, and then a name of your own choosing followed by a pair of parentheses with no spaces before or inside. Then put a colon at the end of that line. For example, to create a simple function named hello( ), type

```
def hello():
```

This is a function, but it doesn't do anything. To make the function do something, you have to write Python code on subsequent lines. To ensure that the new code is "inside" the function, indent each of those lines.

REMEMBER

Indentations matter big time in Python. There is no command that marks the end of a function. All indented lines below the def line are part of that function. The first un-indented line (indented as far out as the def line) is outside the function.

To make this function do something, put an indented line of code under def. We'll start by just having the function print hello. So, type print('Hello') indented under the def line. Now your code looks like this:

```
def hello():
    print('Hello')
```

If you run the code now, nothing obvious will happen on your screen. That's because the code inside a function isn't executed until the function is *called*. You call your own functions the same way you call built-in functions: by writing code that calls the function by name, including the parentheses at the end.

For example, if you're following along, press Enter to add a blank line and then type hello( ) (no spaces in there) and make sure it's *not* indented. (You don't want this code to be indented because it's *calling* the function to execute its code; it's not *part of* the function.) So it looks like this:

```
def hello():
    print('Hello')
hello()
```

Still, nothing happens if you're in a .py file because you've only typed the code so far. For anything to happen, you have to run the code in the usual way in VS Code (if you're using a .py file in VS Code). When the code executes, you should see the output, which is just the word Hello, as shown in Figure 8-1.

```
def hello():
    print('Hello')

hello()

Hello
```

FIGURE 8-1: Writing, and calling, a simple function named hello( ).

Commenting a Function

Comments are always optional in code. But it's customary to make the first line under the def statement a *docstring* (text enclosed in triple quotation marks) that describes what the function does. It's also common to put a comment, preceded by a # sign, to the right of the parentheses in the first line. Because they're just comments, they don't have any effect on what the code does. Comments are just notes to yourself or to programming team members describing what the code is about. Figure 8-2 shows an example of a couple of comments added to our tiny hello() function in the VS Code editor. The first comment, #Practice function, is next to the function name. The next comment is a docstring enclosed in triple quotation marks.

```
hello.py > ...
1    def hello():  # Practice function
2        """ A docstring describing the function """
3        print("Hello, world!")
4
```

FIGURE 8-2: A sample function with a couple of comments added.

Passing Information to a Function

You can pass information to a function for it to work on. To do so, enter a parameter name in the def statement for each piece of information you'll be passing to the function. You can use any name for the parameter, as long as it starts with a letter or underscore, followed by a letter, an underscore, or a number. The name should not contain spaces or punctuation. (Parameter names and variable names follow the same rules.) Ideally, the parameter should describe what's being passed in, for code readability, but you can use generic names like x and y, if you prefer.

Any name you provide as a parameter is local only to that function. For example, if you have a variable named x outside the function and another variable named x inside the function, any changes you make to the x variable inside the function won't affect the x variable outside the function.

The technical term for the way variables work inside functions is *local scope*, meaning that the scope of the variables' existence and influence stays inside the function and does not extend further. Variables created and modified inside a function literally cease to exist the moment the function stops running, and any variables defined outside the function are unaffected by the goings-on inside the function. This is a good thing because when you're writing a function, you don't have to worry about accidentally changing a variable outside the function that happens to have the same name.

Suppose you want the hello function to say Hello to whoever is using the app (and you have access to that information in some variable). To pass the information into the function and use it there, you would do the following:

>> Put a parameter name inside the function's parentheses to act as a placeholder for the incoming information.

>> Inside the function, use that name to work with the information passed in.

For example, suppose you want to pass a person's name into the hello function and then use the name in the print() statement.

You could use any generic name for both the parameter and the function, like this:

```
def hello(x): # Practice function
    """ A docstring describing the function """
    print('Hello ' + x)
```

Inside the parentheses of hello(x), the x is a parameter, a place-holder for whatever is being passed in. Inside the function, that x refers only to the value passed into the function. Any variables named x outside the function are separate from the x used in the parameter name and inside the function.

Generic names don't exactly help make your code easy to understand. It would be better to use a more descriptive name, such as name or even user_name, as in the following:

```
def hello(user_name): # Practice function
    """ A docstring describing the function """
    print('Hello ' + user_name)
```

In the print() function, we added a space after the o in Hello so there'd be a space between Hello and the name in the output.

When a function has a parameter, you have to pass it a value when you call it or it won't work. For example, if you added the parameter to the def statement and still tried to call the function without the parameter, as in the following code, running the code would produce an error:

```
def hello(user_name): # Practice function
    """ A docstring describing the function """
    print('Hello ' + user_name)
hello()
```

The error would read something like the following:

```
hello() missing 1 required positional argument:
  'user_name'
```

which is a major nerd-o-rama way of saying the hello function expected something to be passed into it.

You can use a variable to pass data, too. For example, in the code in Figure 8-3 we stored the string "Alan" in a variable named this_person. Then we call the function using that variable name. Running that code produces Hello Alan, as shown at the bottom of that figure.

```
def hello(user_name):    # Practice function
    """ A docstring describing the function """
    print('Hello ' + user_name)

# Put a string in a variable named this_person.
this_person = 'Alan'
# Pass that variable name to the function.
hello(this_person)
```
```
Hello Alan
```

FIGURE 8-3: Passing data to a function via a variable.

Defining optional parameters with defaults

In the preceding section, we mention that when you call a function that expects parameters without passing those parameters, you get an error. That was a little bit of a lie. You *can* write a function so that passing a parameter is optional so ask ChatGPT how to do this if you need to set defaults.

Passing multiple values to a function

So far in all our examples in this chapter, we've passed just one value to the function. But you can pass as many values as you want. Just provide a parameter name for each value, and separate the names with commas.

For example, suppose you want to pass the user's first name, last name, and maybe a date to the function. You could define those three parameters like this:

```
def hello(fname, lname, datestring): # Practice
    function
        """ A docstring describing the function """
        print('Hello ' + fname + ' ' + lname)
        print('The date is ' + datestring)
```

Note that none of the parameters is optional. So when calling the function, you need to pass three values, such as this:

```
hello('Alan', 'Simpson', '12/31/2024')
```

Figure 8-4 shows an example of executing code with a `hello()` function that accepts three parameters.

```
def hello(fname, lname, datestring): # Practice function
    """ A docstring describing the function """
    print('Hello ' + fname + ' ' + lname)
    print('The date is ' + datestring)

#Test the function
hello("Alan', 'Simpson', '12/31/2024')
```
```
Hello Alan Simpson
The date is 12/31/2024
```

FIGURE 8-4: The `hello` function with three parameters.

If you want to use some (but not all) optional parameters with multiple parameters, make sure the optional ones are the last ones entered. For example, consider the following, which would *not* work:

```
def hello(fname, lname='unknown', datestring):
```

If you try to run this code with that arrangement, you get an error that reads something along the lines of

```
SyntaxError: non-default argument follows default
    argument.
```

This error is trying to tell you that if you want to list both required parameters and optional parameters in a function, you have to put all the required ones first (in any order). Then the optional parameters can be listed after that with their = signs (in any order). So the following would work fine:

```
def hello(fname, lname, datestring=''):
    msg = 'Hello ' + fname + ' ' + lname
    if len(datestring) > 0:
        msg += ' The date is ' + datestring
    print(msg)
```

Logically, the code inside the function does the following:

>> Creates a variable named msg and puts in Hello and the first and last name.

>> If the datestring passed has a length greater than 0, adds "The date is " and that datestring to the msg variable.

>> Prints whatever is in the msg variable at this point.

Figure 8-5 shows two examples of calling this version of the function. The first call passes three values, and the second call passes only two. Both work because the third parameter is optional. The output from the first call is the full output including the date, and the output from the second omits the part about the date.

```
def hello(fname, lname, datestring=''): # Practice function
    """ A docstring describing the function """
    msg = "Hello " + fname + ' ' + lname
    if len(datestring) > 0:
        msg += " The date is " + datestring
    print(msg)

#Test the function
hello('Alan', 'Simpson', '12/31/2024')
hello('Sammy', 'Schmeedeldorp')
```
[3]   ✓ 0.0s

```
Hello Alan Simpson The date is 12/31/2024
Hello Sammy Schmeedeldorp
```

FIGURE 8-5: Calling the hello() function with three parameters, and again with two parameters.

TIP

If you can't remember the syntax for writing functions, just ask GitHub Copilot, ChatGPT, or other AI to write it for you. If you want it to accept parameters, you can specify those, too. For example, telling it to *write a python function named hello that accepts parameters named firstname and lastname* will get you the basic code needed to define the function.

Using keyword arguments (kwargs)

If you've ever looked at the official Python documentation at Python.org, you may have noticed that they throw around the term *kwargs* a lot. That's short for *keyword arguments* and is yet another way to pass data to a function.

The term *argument* is the technical term for "the value you are passing to a function's parameters." So far, we've used strictly positional arguments. For example, consider these three parameters:

```
def hello(fname, lname, datestring=''):
```

As an alternative to relying solely on an argument's position in the code to associate it with a parameter name, you can tell the function what's what by using the syntax *parameter* = *value* in the code calling the function. For example, take a look at this call to hello:

```
hello(datestring='12/31/2019', lname='Simpson',
    fname='Alan')
```

When you run this code, it works fine even though the order of the arguments passed doesn't match the order of the parameter names in the def statement. The value assigned to each parameter name is the name of a variable, not a literal value being passed in.

```
appt_date = '12/30/2019'
last_name = 'Janda'
first_name = 'Kylie'
hello(datestring=appt_date, lname=last_name,
    fname=first_name)
```

Figure 8-6 shows the result of running the code both ways. As you can see, it all works fine. There's no ambiguity about which argument goes with which parameter because the parameter name is specified in the calling code.

Passing in an arbitrary number of arguments

A list provides one way of passing a lot of values into a function. You can also design the function so that it accepts any number of arguments. Note that this method is not particularly faster or better, so use whichever is easiest or makes the most sense. To pass in any number of arguments, use *args as the parameter name, like this:

```
def sorter(*args):
```

```
def hello(fname, lname, datestring=''): # Practice function
    """ A docstring describing the function """
    msg = "Hello " + fname + ' ' + lname
    msg += " The date is " + datestring
    print(msg)

    # Pass in literal kwargs (identify each by parameter name)
    hello(datestring='12/31/2024', lname='Simpson', fname='Alan')

    # Pass in kwargs from variables (identify each by parameter name)
    apt_date = "12/31/2024"
    last_name = "Janda"
    first_name = "Kylie"
    hello(datestring=apt_date, lname=last_name, fname=first_name)

[1]  ✓ 0.0s

... Hello Alan Simpson The date is 12/31/2024
    Hello Kylie Janda The date is 12/31/2024
```

FIGURE 8-6: Calling a function with keyword arguments (kwargs).

Whatever you pass in becomes a tuple named `args` inside the function. Remember, a tuple is an immutable list (a list you can't change). So if you want to change things, you need to copy the tuple to a list and then work on that copy. Here is an example where the code uses the simple statement `newlist = list(args)`. You can read that as *the variable named newlist is a list of all the things that are in the args tuple*. The next line, `newlist.sort()`, sorts the list, and `print` displays the contents of the list:

```
def sorter(*args):
    """ Pass in any number of arguments separated
    by commas
    Inside the function, they treated as a tuple
    named args. """
    # Create a list from the passed-in tuple.
    newlist = list(args)
    # Sort and show the list.
    newlist.sort()
    print(newlist)
```

Figure 8-7 shows an example of running this code with a series of numbers as arguments. As you can see, the resulting list is in sorted order, as expected.

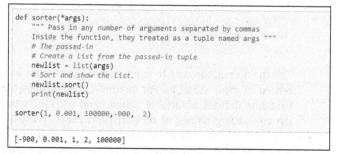

```
def sorter(*args):
    """ Pass in any number of arguments separated by commas
    Inside the function, they treated as a tuple named args """
    # The passed-in
    # Create a list from the passed-in tuple
    newlist = list(args)
    # Sort and show the list.
    newlist.sort()
    print(newlist)

sorter(1, 0.001, 100000,-900,  2)

[-900, 0.001, 1, 2, 100000]
```

FIGURE 8-7: A function accepting any number of arguments with *args.

Returning Values from Functions

So far, all most of our functions have displayed output on the screen so that you can make sure the function works. In real life, it's more common for a function to *return* some value and put it in a variable specified in the calling code. The line that does the returning is typically the last line of the function. That line starts with the word return, followed by a space and the name of the variable (or some expression) that contains the value to be returned.

Here is a variation of the alphabetize function. It contains no print statement. Instead, at the end, it simply returns the alphabetized list (final_list) that the function created:

```
def alphabetize(original_list=[]):
    """ Pass any list in square brackets, displays
    a string with items sorted """
    # Inside the function make a working copy of
    the list passed in.
    sorted_list = original_list.copy()
    # Sort the working copy.
    sorted_list.sort()
    # Make a new empty string for output
    final_list = ''
    # Loop through sorted list and append name and
    comma and space.
    for name in sorted_list:
        final_list += name + ', '
    # Knock off last comma space
```

```
final_list = final_list[:-2]
# Return the alphabetized list.
return final_list
```

The most common way to use functions is to store whatever they return in some variable. For example, in the following code, the first line defines a variable called random_list, which is just a list containing names in no particular order, enclosed in square brackets (which tells Python it's a list). The second line creates a new variable named alpha_list by passing random_list to the alphabetize() function and storing whatever that function returns. The final print statement displays whatever is in the alpha_list variable:

```
random_list = ['McMullen', 'Keaser', 'Maier',
    'Wilson', 'Yudt',
      'Gallagher', 'Jacobs']
alpha_list = alphabetize(random_list)
print(alpha_list)
```

Figure 8-8 shows the result of running the whole kit and caboodle.

```
def alphabetize(original_list=[]):
    """ Pass any list in square brackets. Function returns a sorted list. """
    # Inside the function make a working copy of the list that was passed in.
    sorted_list = original_list.copy()
    # Sort the working copy.
    sorted_list.sort()
    # Make a new empty string for outputcle
    final_list = ""
    # Loop through the sorted list and append name and comma and space
    for name in sorted_list:
        final_list += name + ", "
    # Knock off the last comma and space
    final_list = final_list[:-2]
    # Return the final list
    return(final_list)

# Test the function
random_list=['McMullen','Keaser','Maier','Wilson','Yudt','Gallagher', 'Jacobs']
alpha_list = alphabetize(random_list)
print(alpha_list)
```
[1] ✓ 0.0s
··· Gallagher, Jacobs, Keaser, Maier, McMullen, Wilson, Yudt

FIGURE 8-8: Printing a string returned by the alphabetize() function.

So, there you have it: the ability to create your own custom functions in Python. In real life, any time you find that you need access to the same chunk of code — the same bit of logic — over and over again in your app, don't simply copy and paste that chunk of code over and over. Instead, put the code in a function that you can call by name. That way, if you decide to change the code, you don't have to go digging through your app to find all the places that need changing. Just change it in the function where it's all defined in one place.

Chapter **9**

Sidestepping Errors

W e all want our programs to run perfectly all the time. But sometimes, situations in the real world stop a program from running. The problem isn't with you or your program. Usually, the person using the program did something wrong. Error handling is all about anticipating these problems, catching the error, and then informing users of the problem so that they can fix it.

The techniques we describe here aren't for fixing bugs in your code. You have to fix that type of error yourself. We're talking strictly about errors in the environment in which the program is running, over which you have no control. *Handling* the error is simply a way of replacing the tech-speak error message that Python normally displays, which is meaningless to most people, with a message that tells users in plain English what's wrong and, ideally, how to fix it.

Again, users will be fixing *the environment in which the program is running* — they won't be fixing your code.

Understanding Exceptions

In Python (and all other programming languages) the term *exception* refers to an error in your code, or in the environment in which the code is running — basically anything that prevents the program from running properly. To see a simple example, have your Python app open a file. The syntax for that is easy:

```
name = open(filename)
```

Replace *name* with a name of your own choosing. Replace *filename* with the name of the file. If the file is in the same folder as the code, you don't need to specify a path to the folder because the current folder is assumed.

Figure 9-1 shows an example. We used VS Code for this example so that you can see the contents of the folder in which we worked. The folder contains a file named showfilecontents.py, which is the file that contains the Python code we wrote. The other file is named people.csv.

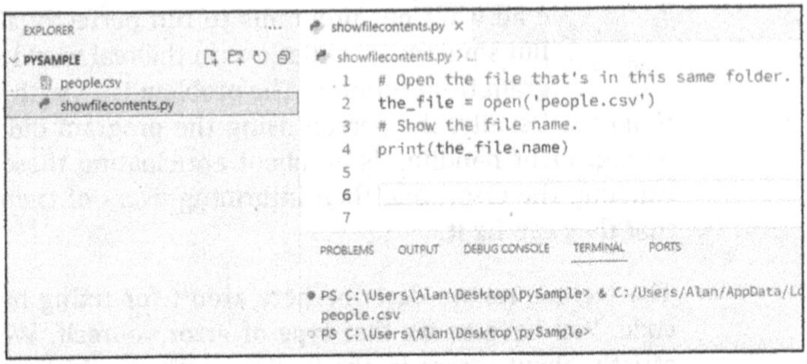

FIGURE 9-1: The showfilecontents.py and people.csv files in a folder in VS Code.

The showcontents.py file contains code. The people.csv file contains data (information about people). Figure 9-2 shows the content of the people.csv file in Excel (top), so that it's easy for you to read, and in a text editor (bottom), which is how it looks to Python and other languages. The file's content doesn't matter much right now; what you're discovering here will work in any external file.

	A	B	C	D	E
1	Username	FirstName	LastName	Role	DateJoined
2	Rambo	Rocco	Moe	0	3/1/2019
3	Ann	Annie	Angst	0	6/4/2019
4	Wil	Wilbur	Blomgren	0	2/28/2019
5	Lupe	Lupe	Gomez	1	4/2/2019
6	Ina	Ina	Kumar	1	1/15/2019
7					

people.csv

```
1  Username,FirstName,LastName,Role,DateJoined
2  Rambo,Rocco,Moe,0,3/1/2019
3  Ann,Annie,Angst,0,6/4/2019
4  Wil,Wilbur,Blomgren,0,2/28/2019
5  Lupe,Lupe,Gomez,1,4/2/2019
6  Ina,Ina,Kumar,1,1/15/2019
7
```

FIGURE 9-2: The contents of the people.csv file in Excel (top) and a text editor (bottom).

The Python code is just two lines (excluding the comments), as follows:

```
# Open file that's in this same folder.
the_file = open('people.csv')
# Show the filename.
print(the_file.name)
```

The first line of code opens the file named people.csv. The second line of code displays the filename (people.csv) on the screen. Running that simple showfilecontents.py app (by right-clicking its name in VS Code and choosing Run Python File in Terminal) displays people.csv on the screen — assuming that a file named people.csv exists in the folder to open. This assumption is where exception handling comes in.

Suppose that for reasons beyond your control, the people.csv file isn't there because some person or automated procedure failed to put it there. Or perhaps someone misspelled the filename. It's easy to accidentally type, say, .cvs rather than .csv for the filename. There are many situations that might make the file unavailable. Running the app when the file is unavailable *raises an exception* (which in English means "displays an error message"), as you can see in the Terminal pane at the bottom of Figure 9-3. The exception reads as follows:

```
Traceback (most recent call last):
  File "c:/Users/acsimpson/Desktop/exceptions/
  showfilecontents.py", line 2,
 in <module>
    the_file = open('people.csv')
FileNotFoundError: [Errno 2] No such file or
  directory: 'people.csv'
```

FIGURE 9-3: The showfilecontents.py file raises an exception.

Traceback is a reference to the fact that if there were multiple exceptions, they'd all be listed, with the most recent listed first. More specifically, if there are multiple function calls leading to the error, Traceback shows you the history of those calls, with the most recent call first. In this case, there is just one exception. The File part tells you where the exception occurred, in line 2 of the showfilecontents.py file. The following part shows you the line of code that caused the error:

```
the_file = open('people.csv')
```

And finally, the exception itself is described:

```
FileNotFoundError: [Errno 2] No such file or
    directory: 'people.csv'
```

The generic name for this type of error is FileNotFoundError. Many exceptions are also associated with a number (ERRNO 2 in this example). But the number can vary depending on the operating system environment, so it's typically not used for handling errors. In this case, the main error is FileNotFoundError, and the fact that's its ERRNO 2 where I'm sitting right now doesn't matter.

The last part tells you *exactly* what went wrong: No such file or directory: 'people.csv.' In other words, Python can't do the open('people.csv') business because there is no file named people.csv in the current folder.

You could correct this problem by changing the code, but .csv is a common file extension for files that contain comma-separated values. It would make more sense to change the name of people. cvs to people.csv so that it matches what the program is looking for, and the .csv extension is well known.

Handling Errors Gracefully

The best way to handle a file-not-found error is to replace what Python normally displays with something the person using the app is more likely to understand. To do that, you can code a *try . . . except block* using this basic syntax:

```
try:
    The things you want the code to do
except Exception:
    What to do if it can't do what you want it to
    do
```

Here's how you can rewrite the showfilecontents.py code to handle a missing (or misspelled) file error:

```
try:
    # Open file and show its name.
    the_file = open('people.csv')
    print(the_file.name)
except Exception:
    print("Sorry, I don't see a file named people.
    csv here")
```

Because the file that the app is supposed to open may be missing, you start with try: and then attempt to open the file under that. If the file opens, the `print()` statement runs and displays the filename. But if trying to open the file raises an exception, the program doesn't bomb and display a generic error message. Instead, it displays a message that the average computer user can understand, as shown in Figure 9-4.

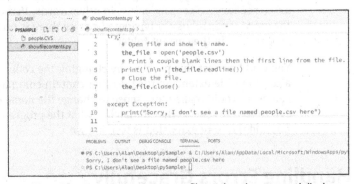

FIGURE 9-4: The `showfilecontents.py` file catches the error and displays a friendly message.

Being Specific about Exceptions

Our previous code example handled the file-not-found error gracefully. But a larger app might have many places where there's a potential for error, and you want to handle each error differently. To do so, you can define multiple error handlers, as we discuss next.

Suppose that you manually fix the filename so that it's `people.csv` as originally intended. As shown previously, when you run the code and there's no error, the output is just the filename. Below the line that prints the filename, we've added another line of code:

```
try:
    # Open file and show its name.
    the_file = open('people.csv')
    print(the_file.name)
    print(the_file.wookems())
except Exception:
    print("Sorry, I don't see a file named people.
  csv here")
```

When you run this code, the filename isn't a problem, so the output displays people.csv, as you'd expect. However, the next line of code, print(the_file.wookems()), throws an error because we haven't defined a method named wookems(). Unfortunately, the error message is still the same as it was before, even though the cause of the error is that there is no method in Python named .wookems():

```
people.csv
Sorry, I don't see a file named people.csv here
```

So why is the error message saying that the file named people.csv wasn't found, when we know it *was* found and that the next line of code is causing the error? The problem is in the except Exception: line, which says "if *any* exception is raised in this try block, do the code under the except line."

To clean up this problem, you need to replace Exception: with the specific exception you want Python to catch. But how do you know what that specific exception is? Easy. The exception raised with no exception handing is

```
FileNotFoundError: [Errno 2] No such file or
    directory: 'people.csv'
```

The first word is the name of the exception that you can use in place of the generic Exception name, like this:

```
try:
    # Open file and show its name.
    the_file = open('people.csv')
    print(the_file.name)
    print(the_file.wookems())
except FileNotFoundError:
    print("Sorry, I don't see a file named people.
  csv here")
```

Granted, isolating the file-not-found error doesn't do anything to help with the bad method name. However, the bad method name isn't an exception; it's a programming error that needs to be corrected in the code by replacing .wookems() with the method name you want to use. At least the error message you see isn't the misleading Sorry, I don't see a file named `people.csv here` error. The code works normally and therefore displays the filename when instructed. Then when it reaches the line that contains the bad `.wookems()` method, it throws an error — but not an error related to the filename not being found. It displays the correct error message for this error, `object has no attribute 'wookems'`, as shown in Figure 9-5.

```
EXPLORER                    ...      showfilecontents.py  ×
PYSAMPLE                            showfilecontents.py > ...
   people.csv                          1    try:
   showfilecontents.py                 2        # Open file and show its name.
                                       3        the_file = open('people.csv')
                                       4        print(the_file.name)
                                       5        print(the_file.wookems)
                                       6
                                       7    except FileNotFoundError:
                                       8        print("Sorry, I don't see a file named people.csv here")
                                       9
                                      10

PROBLEMS   OUTPUT   DEBUG CONSOLE   TERMINAL   PORTS

 PS C:\Users\Alan\Desktop\pySample> & C:/Users/Alan/AppData/Local/Microsoft/Windo
 people.csv
 Traceback (most recent call last):
   File "c:\Users\Alan\Desktop\pySample\showfilecontents.py", line 5, in <module>
     print(the_file.wookems)
           ^^^^^^^^^^^^^^^^^
 AttributeError: '_io.TextIOWrapper' object has no attribute 'wookems'
 PS C:\Users\Alan\Desktop\pySample> []
```

FIGURE 9-5: The correct error message is displayed.

Again, if you're thinking about handling the `.wookems` error, that's not an exception for which you'd write an exception handler. Exceptions occur when something *outside* the program upon which the program depends isn't available. Programming errors, such as nonexistent method names, are errors inside the program and have to be corrected there by the programmer who wrote the code.

TIP

Github Copilot, ChatGPT, Claude.ai, and other generative AI products can write Python exception handlers for you. Just ask the AI to *write a Python exception handler for file not found*. But replace the words *file not found* with whatever exception you're trying to handle.

Keeping Your App from Crashing

You can stack up except: statements in a try block to handle different errors. Just be aware that when the exception occurs, it looks at each one starting at the top. If it finds a handler that matches the exception, it raises that one. If some exception occurred that you didn't handle, you get the standard Python error message. But there's a way around that, too.

If you want to avoid all Python error messages, you can start the last exception handler in the code with `except Exception:`. That line means "If the error that occurred wasn't already handled by one of the previous exceptions, use the exception handler instead."

Adding an else to the Mix

In the previous example, we used one error handler to handle file-not-found errors, and a second handler for everything else. But in real life, you may have to handle many more kinds of errors. So there may be `except:` blocks for various errors. But what if none of the errors you're trying to catch occurs? In that case, you want code execution to proceed normally. You can add an `else:` block to your code to handle the situation when there is no error to catch.

```
try:
    The thing that might cause an exception
catch a common exception:
    Explain the problem
catch Exception as e:
    Show the generic error message
else:
    Continue on here only if no exceptions raised
```

If you convert this code to plain English, the logic of the flow is as follows:

Try to open the file.

If the file isn't there, tell the user and stop.

If there's some other error, show the generic error message and stop.

Otherwise

Go on with the rest of the code.

By limiting `try:` to the one thing that's most likely to raise an exception, we can stop the code dead in its tracks before it tries to go any further. But if no exception is raised, the code continues on normally, below the `else`, where the previous exception handlers don't matter anymore. Here is all the code with comments explaining what's going on:

```python
try:
    # Open the file named people.csv
    the_file = open('people.csv')
# Watch for common error and stop program if it
  happens.
except FileNotFoundError:
    print("Sorry, I don't see a file named people.
  csv here")
# Catch any unexpected error.
except Exception as err:
    print(err)
# Otherwise, if nothing bad has happened by now,
  just keep going.
else:
    # File must be open by now if we got here.
    print('\n') # Print a blank line.
    # Print each line from the file.
    for one_line in the_file:
        print(one_line)
    the_file.close()
    print("Success!")
```

As always with Python, indentations matter a lot. Make sure you indent your own code as shown in this chapter. Otherwise, your code will not work right.

Figure 9-6 also shows all the code and the results of running that code in VS Code.

```
showfilecontents.py > ...
  1   try:
  2       # Open the file named people.csv
  3       the_file = open('people.csv')
  4   # Watch for common error and stop program if it happens.
  5   except FileNotFoundError:
  6       print("Sorry, I don't see a file named people.csv here")
  7   # Catch any unexpected error and stop the program if one happens.
  8   except Exception as err:
  9       print(err)
 10   # Otherwise, if nothing bad has happened by now, just keep going.
 11   else:
 12       # File must be open by now if we got here.
 13       print('\n') # Print a blank line.
 14       # Print each line from the file.
 15       for one_line in the_file:
 16           print(one_line)
 17       the_file.close()
 18       print("Success!")
 19
```

```
PROBLEMS   OUTPUT   DEBUG CONSOLE   TERMINAL   PORTS

PS C:\Users\Alan\Desktop\pySample> & C:/Users/Alan/AppData/Local/Microsoft/WindowsApps/pytho

Username,FirstName,LastName,DateJoined

Rambo,Rocco,Moe,3/1/2019

Ann,Annie,Angst,6/4/2019

Wil,Wilbur,Blomgren,2/28/2019

Lupe,Lupe,Gomez,4/2/2019

Ina,Ina,Kumar,1/15/2019

Success!
```

FIGURE 9-6: Code with try, exception handlers, and an else: block for when there are no exceptions.

Using try ... except ... else ... finally

If you look at the complete syntax for Python exception handling, you'll see one more option at the end, like this:

```
try:
    try to do this
except:
    if x happens, stop here
except Exception as e:
    if something else bad happens, stop here
```

```
else:
    if no exceptions, continue on normally here
finally:
    do this code no matter what happened above
```

The `finally` code is executed when the try block ends *no matter what*. For example, if you're inside a function and an `except` block uses `return` to exit the function, the `finally` code *still* executes. Without that kind of feature, the `finally` block would be the equivalent of putting its code after and outside the try block.

To illustrate, the upcoming code sets a variable named `file_is_open` to `False`. Then it attempts to open the file. If the file cannot be opened, the first `except:` block catches the error, so the program doesn't crash. The `file_is_open` variable remains set to `True`.

If the file can be opened, the `else:` block executes, sets the `file_is_open` variable to `True`, and then displays the file's contents on the screen.

Finally (in the `finally:` block), the code checks to see if `is_file_open` is `True`, and if it is `True`, it closes the file. So regardless of the situation, the program will run without crashing and will also ensure that the file is closed before moving on to the next code.

```
# A variable that starts out False.
file_is_open = False

try:
    # Open the file named people.csv
    the_file = open("people.csv")

# Watch for common error and stop program if it
    happens.
except FileNotFoundError:
    print("Sorry, I don't see a file named people.
    csv here")

# Otherwise, if nothing bad has happened by now,
    just keep going.
```

```
else:
    # File must be open by now. Set the open
status to True.
    file_is_open = True
    # Show the file contents.
    for one_line in the_file:
        print(one_line)

finally:
    # This executes no matter what. So if the file
is open, it's closed.
    if file_is_open:
        the_file.close()
    print("File is closed now")
```

TIP

If you forget the syntax for Python try ... catch blocks, just ask Copilot, Claude.ai, or other generative AI to *write python code for a try, except, else, finally block.* That will get you the basic syntax typed up in an example.

These examples illustrate that you can control exactly what happens in a small part of a program that is vulnerable to user errors or other outside exceptions, while allowing other code to run normally.

Raising Your Own Exceptions

Python has lots of built-in exceptions for recognizing and identifying errors, as you'll see while writing and testing code, especially when you're first learning. However, you aren't limited to the built-in exceptions. If your app has a vulnerability that isn't covered by the built-in exceptions, you can invent your own. Ask ChatGPT for an example of how to raise your own exception in Python.

The general syntax for raising your own error is

```
raise error
```

Replace *error* with the name of the known error that you want to raise (such as FileNotFoundError). Or, if the error isn't covered by one of the built-in errors, you can just use `raise Exception`, and that will execute whatever is under `catch Exception:` in your code.

So as you can see, exception handling lets you plan for errors caused by vulnerabilities in your code. We're referring not to bugs in your code or coding errors but to outside resources that the program needs to run correctly.

When outside resources are missing or insufficient, you don't have to let the program just crash and display a nerd-o-rama error message that will baffle your users. Instead, you can catch the exception and show users some text that tells them exactly what's wrong, which will help them fix the problem and run the program again, successfully this time. That's what exception handling is all about.

Chapter **10**

Working with External Files

Pretty much everything stored in your computer, be it a document, program, movie, photograph, and more, is stored in a file. Most files are organized into *folders* (also called *directories*). You can browse through folders and files by using Finder (on a Mac) or File Explorer or Windows Explorer (in Windows).

Python offers many tools for creating, reading from, and writing to many different kinds of files. In this chapter, you learn the most important skills for using Python code to work with files.

Understanding Text and Binary Files

There are basically two types of files:

» **Text file:** Contains plain text characters. When you open a text file in a text editor, it displays human-readable content. The text may not be in a language you know or understand, but you will see mostly normal characters that you can type at any keyboard.

>> **Binary file:** Stores information in bytes that aren't quite so human readable.

Figure 10-1 lists examples of different kinds of text and binary files, some of which you may have worked with before. Other files types are available; these are among the most widely used.

Text File
- **Plain text:** .txt, .csv
- **Source code:** .py, .html, .css, .js
- **Data:** .json, .xml

Binary File
- **Executable:** .exe, .dmg, .bin
- **Images:** .jpg, .png, .gif, .tiff, .ico
- **Video:** .mp4, .m4v, .mp4, .mov
- **Audio:** .aif, .mp3, .mpa, .wav
- **Compressed:** .zip, .deb, .tar.gz
- **Font:** .woff, .otf, .ttf
- **Document:** .pdf, .docx, .xlsx

FIGURE 10-1: Common text and binary files.

You can use VS Code or almost any coding editor to write your Python code. We use VS Code in this chapter simply because its Explorer pane (on the left, when it's open) displays the contents of the folder in which you're currently working.

Opening and Closing Files

To open a file from a Python app, use this syntax:

```
open(filename.ext[,mode])
```

Replace *filename.ext* with the filename of the file you want to open. If the file is not in the same directory as the Python code, you need to specify a path to the file. For example, if you're using Windows and you want to open the foo.txt on your desktop and your user account name is Alan, you'd use the path C:/Users/Alan/Desktop/foo.txt rather than the more common Windows syntax with backslashes (C:\Users\Alan\Desktop\foo.txt).

The *,mode* is optional (as indicated by the square brackets). Use it to specify what kind of access you want your app to have, using the following single-character abbreviations:

>> **r: (Read):** Opens the file but does not allow Python to make any changes. This is the default mode and is used if you

don't specify a mode. If the file doesn't exist, Python raises a FileNotFoundError exception.

>> **r+: (Read/Write):** Opens the file and allows Python to read and write to the file.

>> **a: (Append):** Opens the file and allows Python to add content to the end of the file but not change existing content. If the file doesn't exist, this mode creates the file.

>> **w: (Write):** Opens the file and overwrites its contents, or creates the file if it doesn't exist.

>> **x: (Create):** Creates the file if it doesn't already exist.

You can also specify the type of file you're opening or creating. If you already specified one of the preceding modes, just add this specification as another letter. If you use just one of the following letters on its own, the file opens in Read mode:

>> **t: (Text):** Opens the file as a text file and allows Python to read and write text.

>> **b: (Binary):** Opens the file as a binary file and allows Python to read and write bytes.

You can use the open method in basically two ways. With one syntax, you assign a variable name to the file, and you use this variable name in code to refer to the file:

```
var = open(filename.ext[,mode])
```

Replace *var* with a name of your choosing (though it's common in Python to use just the letter f as the name).

After the file is open, you can access its content in a few ways, as we discuss a little later in the chapter. For now, we simply copy everything in the file to a variable named *filecontents*, and then we display this content using a simple print() function. So to open quotes.txt, read in all its content, and display that content on the screen, use this code:

```
f = open('quotes.txt')
filecontents = f.read()
print(filecontents)
```

With this method, the file remains open until you specifically close it using the file variable name and the .close() method, like this:

```
f.close()
```

Make sure that your apps close any files they no longer need open. Failure to do so allows open file handlers to accumulate, which can eventually cause the app to throw an exception and crash, perhaps even corrupting some of the open files along the way.

The second way to open a file is by using a context manager or contextual coding. *Contextual coding* starts with the word with. You still assign a variable name, but you do so near the end of the line. The last thing on the line is a colon, which marks the beginning of the with block. All indented code below that is assumed to be relevant to the context of the open file (like code indented inside a loop). At the end of contextual coding, you don't need to close the file because Python does it automatically:

```
# --------------- Contextual syntax
with open('quotes.txt') as f:
    filecontents = f.read()
    print(filecontents)

# The unindented line below is outside the with...
   block;
print('File is closed: ', f.closed)
```

For the rest of this chapter, we stick with contextual syntax because it's generally the preferred and recommended syntax and a good habit to acquire right from the start.

Reading a File's Contents

Previously in this chapter, you saw how you can use .read() to read the contents of an open file. But that's not the only way to read a file. You have three choices:

>> read([size]): Reads the entire file if you leave the parentheses empty. If you specify a size inside the

parentheses, it reads that many characters (for a text file) or that many bytes (for a binary file).

≫ readline(): Reads one line of the contents from a text file — the line ends wherever there's a newline character. (The newline character, \n, ends the line that's displayed and moves the cursor down to the next line.)

≫ readlines(): Reads all the lines of a text file into a list.

Both the read() and readline() methods read in the entire file simultaneously. The only difference is that read reads in the file as one big chunk of data, whereas readlines() reads in the file one line at a time and stores each line as an item in a list. For example, the following code opens quotes.txt, reads in all the contents, and then displays it:

```
with open('quotes.txt') as f:
    # Read in entire file
    content = f.read()
    print(content)
```

The content variable stores a copy of everything from the text file. We print the variable to display its contents. The newline character at the end of each line in the file starts a new line on the screen when printing.

Here is the same code using readlines() rather than read:

```
with open('quotes.txt') as f:
    content = f.readlines()
    print(content)
```

The output from this code is

```
["I've had a perfectly wonderful evening, but this
    wasn't it.\n",
'Groucho Marx\n', 'The difference between
    stupidity and genius is that
genius has its limits.\n', 'Albert Einstein\n',
    'We are all here on earth to
help others; what on earth the others are here
    for, I have no idea.\n',
```

```
'W. H. Auden\n', 'Ending a sentence with a
   preposition is something up with
which I will not put.\n', 'Winston Churchill\n']
```

The square brackets surrounding the output tell you that it's a
list. Each item in the list is surrounded by quotation marks and
separated by commas. The \n at the end of each item is the newline character that ends the line in the file.

Unlike readlines() (plural), readline() reads just one line from
the file. The line extends from the current position in the file to the
next newline character. Executing another readline() reads the
next line in the file, and so forth. For example, suppose you run
this code:

```
with open('quotes.txt') as f:
    content = f.readline()
    print(content)
```

The output is

```
I've had a perfectly wonderful evening, but this
   wasn't it.
```

Executing another readline() after this would read the next
line. As you may guess, when it comes to readline() and
readlines(), you're likely to want to use loops to access all the
data in a way that gives you more control.

Looping through a File

You can loop through a file using either readlines() or
readline(). The readlines() method always reads in the file as
a whole. So if the file is very large, your computer may run out of
memory (RAM) before the file has been read in. But if you know
the size of the file and it's relatively small (maybe a few thousand
or fewer rows of data), readlines() is a speedy way to get all the
data. That data will be in a list, so you will loop through the list
rather than the file.

Looping with readlines()

When you read a file with readlines(), you read the entire file in one fell swoop as a list. So you don't really loop through the file one row at a time. Rather, you loop through the list of items that readlines() stores in memory. The code to do so looks like this:

```
with open('quotes.txt') as f:
    # Reads in all lines first, then loops
    through.
    for one_line in f.readlines():
        print(one_line)
```

If you run this code, the output will be double-spaced because each list item ends with a newline, and then print normally adds its own newline with each pass through the loop. If you want to retain the single spacing, add end='' to the print statement (make sure you use two single or double quotation marks with no spaces after =).

Looping with readline()

If you aren't too sure about the size of the file you're reading or the amount of RAM in the computer running your app, using readlines() to read in an entire file can be risky. If there isn't enough memory to hold the entire file, the app will crash when it runs out of memory. To play it safe, you can loop through the file one line at a time so that only one line of the contents from the file is in memory at any given time.

To use this method, you open the file, read one line, and put it in a variable. Then loop through the file *as long as* (while) the variable isn't empty. Because each line in the file contains some text, the variable won't be empty until after the last line is read. Here is the code for this approach to looping:

```
with open('quotes.txt') as f:
    one_line = f.readline()
    while one_line:
        print(one_line, end='')
        one_line = f.readline()
```

For larger files, this method is the way to go because at no point are you reading in the entire file. The only potential problem is forgetting to include .readline() inside the loop to advance to the next row. If you forget the readline(), you end up in an infinite loop that prints the first line over and over. If you ever find yourself in this situation, press Ctrl+C in the Terminal pane where the code is running to stop the loop.

You can accomplish the same format, in which you indent the name under each quote and add a blank line, by using .readline() in Python. In your code, start a counter at 1. Create a loop that reads one row at a time from the text file. Within that loop, increment your counter variable by 1 with each pass through the loop. Then indent and do the extra space on even-numbered lines, like this:

```
# Store a number to use as a loop counter.
counter = 1
# Open the file.
with open('quotes.txt') as f:
    # Read one line from the file.
    one_line = f.readline()
    # As long as there are lines to read...
    while one_line:
        # If the counter is an even number, print
a couple spaces.
        if counter % 2 == 0:
            print('   ' + one_line)
        # Otherwise print with no newline at the
end.
        else:
            print(one_line, end='')
        # Increment the counter
        counter += 1
        # Read the next line.
        one_line = f.readline()
```

The output from this loop is the same as for the second readlines() loop, in which each author's name is indented and followed by an extra blank line caused by using print() without the end=''.

You can use generative AI to write code for opening and looping through files. For example, ask Copilot or ChatGPT to *write python code to open a text file named whatever.txt and loop through its contents. Include exception handler for file not found.* Then just modify the code it generates to suit your needs.

Appending versus overwriting files

WARNING

Anytime you work with files, it's important to understand the difference between *write* and *append*. If a file contains information and you open it in write mode and then write to it, your new content will overwrite (replace) whatever is already in the file. There is no undo for this. So if the content of the file is important, you want to make sure you don't make that mistake. To add content to the end of a file, open the file in append (a) mode, and then use .write to write to the file.

Using tell() to determine the pointer location

When you loop through a file, its contents are read top to bottom and left to right. Python maintains a pointer to keep track of where it is in the file. When you're reading a text file with readline(), the pointer is always the character position of the next line in the file.

Moving the pointer with seek()

Whereas the tell() method tells you where the pointer is in an external file, the seek() method enables you to reposition the pointer. The syntax is

```
file.seek(position[,whence])
```

Replace *file* with the variable name of the open file. Replace *position* to indicate where you want to put the pointer. For example, 0 moves the pointer back to the top of the file. The *whence* is optional; you can use it to indicate where in the file to set the pointer position. Your choices are

>> 0: Set the position relative to the start of the file.

>> 1: Set the position relative to the current pointer position.

>> 2: Set the position relative to the end of the file. Use a negative number for *position*.

If you omit the *whence* value, it defaults to 0.

By far the most common use of seek is to just reset the pointer back to the top of the file for another pass through the file. The syntax for this is simply .seek(0).

Reading and Copying a Binary File

Suppose you have an app that changes a binary file, and you want to always work with a copy of the original file to play it safe. Binary files can be huge, so rather than opening it all at once and risking running out of memory, you can read it in chunks and write it out in chunks. Binary files do not have human-readable content. Nor do they have lines of text. So readline() and readlines() aren't a good choice for looping through binary files, but you can use .read() with a specified size.

Figure 10-2 shows the binarycopy.py file, which makes a copy of any binary file. We take you through that code step-by-step so that you can understand how it works.

```
binarycopy.py > ...
1   # Specify the file to copy
2   file_to_copy = 'happy_pickle.jpg'
3   #Create new file nane wuth _copy before the extension.
4   name_parts = file_to_copy.split('.')
5   new_file = name_parts[0] + '_copy.' + name_parts[1]
6   # Open the priginal file as read-only binary.
7   with open(file_to_copy,'rb') as original_file:
8       # Create or open file to copy into.
9       with open(new_file,'wb') as copy_to:
10          # Grab a chunk of the original file (4MB).
11          chunk=original_file.read(4096)
12          # Loop though until no more chunks.
13          while len(chunk) > 0:
14              copy_to.write(chunk)
15              # Make sure you read the next chunk in this loop.
16              chunk = original_file.read(4096)
17
18  # Close is automatic after loops, show done message.
19  print('Done!')
```

FIGURE 10-2: The binarycopy.py file copies any binary file.

Figure 10-3 shows the results of running the code. The Terminal pane simply shows Done!. But as you can see, there's now a file named happy_pickle_copy.jpg in the folder. Opening this file will prove that it is a copy of the original file.

```
EXPLORER                        ● binarycopy.py ×    □ happy_pickle.jpg
▲ OPEN EDITORS            1      # Specify the file to copy.
  ✖ ● binarycopy.py       2      file_to_copy = 'happy_pickle.jpg'
    □ happy_pickle.jpg     3
▲ SAMPLE FILES            4      # Create new file name with _copy before the extension.
  ● binarycopy.py         5      name_parts = file_to_copy.split('.')
  □ happy_pickle_copy.jpg  6      new_file = name_parts[0] + '_copy.' + name_parts[1]
  □ happy_pickle.jpg      7
  ▤ names.txt             8      # Open the original file as read-only binary.
  ▤ quotes.txt            9      with open(file_to_copy, 'rb') as original_file:
  ▦ sample.csv            10
  ▦ sample.xlsx           11         # Create or open file to copy into.
                          12         with open(new_file, 'wb') as copy_to:
                          13
                          14             # Grab a chunk of original file (4MB).
                          15             chunk = original_file.read(4096)
                          16
                          17             # Loop through until no more chunks.
                          18             while len(chunk) > 0:
                          19
                          20                 copy_to.write(chunk)
                          21                 # Make sure you read in the next chunk in this loop.
                          22                 chunk = original_file.read(4096)
                          23
                          24     # Close is automatic after loops, show done message.
                          25     print('Done!')
                          26

PROBLEMS    OUTPUT    DEBUG CONSOLE    TERMINAL

(base) C:\Users\acsimpson\Desktop\sample files>C:/Users/acsimpson/AppData/Local
Done!
```

FIGURE 10-3: Running binarycopy.py added happy_pickle_copy.jpg to the folder.

Chapter **11**

Juggling JSON Data

J avaScript Object Notation (JSON) is a common marshalling format for object-oriented data. *Marshalling format* generally means a format used to send data from one computer to another. However, some databases, such as the free Realtime Database at Google's Firebase, store the data in JavaScript Object Notation format as well. The name *JavaScript* at the front sometimes throws people off, especially when you're using Python, not JavaScript, to write your code. But don't worry. The format just got its start in the JavaScript world and is now a widely known general-purpose format used with all kinds of computers and programming languages.

In this chapter, you learn exactly what JSON is, as well as how to export and import data to and from JSON. If you find that all the buzzwords surrounding JSON make you uncomfortable, again, don't worry. We get through all the jargon first. As you'll see, JSON data is formatted almost the same way as Python data dictionaries, so there won't be a lot of new stuff to learn. Also, you already have the free Python JSON module, which makes it even easier to work with JSON data.

Organizing JSON Data

JSON data is roughly the equivalent of a data dictionary in Python, which makes JSON files fairly easy to work with. JSON data is probably easiest to understand when it's compared to tabular data. For instance, Figure 11-1 shows some tabular data in an Excel worksheet. Figure 11-2 shows the same data converted to JSON format. Each row of data in the Excel sheet has been converted to a dictionary of *key:value* pairs in the JSON file. And there are, of course, lots of curly braces to indicate that the data is an object.

	A	B	C	D	E
1	Full Name	Birth Year	Date Joined	Is Active	Balance
2	Angst, Annie	1982	1/11/2011	TRUE	$300.00
3	Bónañas, Barry	1973	2/11/2012	FALSE	-$123.45
4	Schadenfreude, Sandy	2004	3/3/2003	TRUE	$0.00
5	Weltschmerz, Wanda	1995	4/24/1994	FALSE	$999,999.99
6	Malaise, Mindy	2006	5/5/2005	TRUE	$454.01
7	O'Possum, Ollie	1987	7/27/1997	TRUE	-$1,000.00
8					
9	Pusillanimity, Pamela	1979	8/8/2008	TRUE	$12,345.67

FIGURE 11-1: Some data in an Excel spreadsheet.

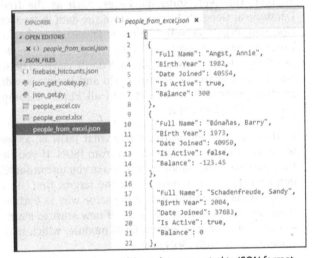

FIGURE 11-2: Excel spreadsheet data converted to JSON format.

To convert existing Excel data to JSON, choose File ⇨ Export or File ⇨ Save As from Excel's menu and export to CSV (Comma Delimited). You can use similar techniques to export CSV from Google Sheets and Apple's Numbers app. After you have a CSV file, you can use the convertcsv.com website to convert that to JSON. Look for the Convert CSV to JSON option at the site, and follow the onscreen instructions.

Exporting data from Excel is just one way to create a JSON file. You can also create a *keyed JSON file,* in which each chunk of data has a single key that uniquely identifies it. (No other dictionary in the same file can have the same key.) The key can be a number or text; it doesn't really matter which, as long as it's unique to each item. When you're downloading JSON files created by someone else, it's not unusual for the file to be keyed. For example, on Alan's personal website, he uses the free Google Firebase Realtime Database to count hits per page and other information about each page. The Realtime Database stores the data as shown in Figure 11-3. Those weird things like *-LAOqOxg6kmP4jhnjQXS* are all keys that the Firebase generates automatically for each item of data to guarantee uniqueness. The + sign next to each key allows you to expand and collapse the information under each key.

FIGURE 11-3: Some data in a Google Firebase Realtime Database.

Understanding Serialization

When it comes to JSON, the first buzzword you have to learn is serialization. *Serialization* is the process of converting an object (such as a Python dictionary) into a stream of bytes or characters that can be sent across a wire, stored in a file or database, or stored in memory. The main purpose is to save all the information in an object in a way that can be retrieved easily on any other computer. The process of converting the information back to an object is called *deserialization*. To keep things simple, you may just consider using these definitions:

>> **Serialize:** Convert an object to a string.

>> **Deserialize:** Convert a string to an object.

The Python standard library includes a `json` module that helps you work with JSON files. Because it's part of the standard library, you just have to put `import json` near the top of your code to access its capabilities. The four main methods for serializing and deserializing `json` are summarized in Table 11-1.

TABLE 11-1 Python JSON Methods for Serializing and Deserializing JSON Data

Method	Purpose
`json.dump()`	Write (serialize) Python data to a JSON file (or stream).
`json.dumps()`	Write (serialize) a Python object to a JSON string.
`json.load()`	Load (deserialize) JSON from a file or similar object.
`json.loads()`	Load (deserialize) JSON data from a string.

Data types in JSON are similar but not identical to data types in Python. Table 11-2 lists how data types are converted between the two languages when serializing and deserializing.

TABLE 11-2 **Python and JSON Data Conversions**

Python	JSON
Dict	Object
list, tuple	Array
Str	String
int and float	Number
True	True
False	False
None	Null

Loading Data from JSON Files

To load data from JSON files, make sure you import json near the top of the code. Then you can use a regular file open() method to open the file. As with other kinds of files, you can add encoding = "utf-8" if you need to preserve non-ASCII characters in the data. You can also use newline="" to avoid bringing in the newline character at the end of each row. The newline character isn't really part of the data; it's a hidden character to end the line when displaying the data on the screen.

WARNING

When experimenting with this code, never name your app json.py. That will change the meaning of import json near the top of the code, and cause the app to show strange error messages when you try to test your code.

To load the JSON data into Python, come up with a variable name to hold the data (we use people). Then use json.load() to load the file contents into the variable, like this:

```
import json
# This is the Excel data (no keys)
filename = 'people_from_excel.json'
# Open the file (standard file open stuff)
with open(filename, 'r', encoding='utf-8',
    newline='') as f:
```

```
# Load the whole json file into an object
named people
  people = json.load(f)
```

Running this code doesn't display anything on the screen. However, you can explore the people object in a number of ways by using un-indented print() statements below the last line. For example, the following displays everything in the people variable:

```
print(people)
```

The output starts and ends with square brackets ([]), which tell you that people is a list. To verify that it's a list, you can run this line of code:

```
print(type(people))
```

Python displays the following:

```
<class 'list'>
```

This line tells you that the object is an instance of the list class. In other words, it's a list object, although most people would just call it a list.

Because the object is a list, you can loop through it. Within the loop, you can display the type of each item, like this:

```
for p in people:
    print(type(p))
```

The output follows:

```
<class 'dict'>
<class 'dict'>
<class 'dict'>
<class 'dict'>
<class 'dict'>
<class 'dict'>
<class 'dict'>
```

This is useful information because it tells you that each of the "people" (which we've abbreviated as p in that code) in the list is a Python dictionary. So within the loop, you can isolate each value by its key. For example, take a look at this code:

```
for p in people:
    print(p['Full Name'], p['Birth Year'], p['Date
    Joined'],
           p['Is Active'], p['Balance'])
```

Running this code displays all the data in the JSON file, as in the following. This data came from the Excel spreadsheet shown previously in Figure 11-1.

```
Angst, Annie 1982 40554 True 300
Bónañas, Barry 1973 40950 False -123.45
Schadenfreude, Sandy 2004 37683 True 0
Weltschmerz, Wanda 1995 34448 False 999999.99
Malaise, Mindy 2006 38477 True 454.01
O'Possum, Ollie 1987 35638 True -1000
Pusillanimity, Pamela 1979 39668 True 12345.67
```

TIP

If all the coding for opening and looping through a JSON file is too complicated, remember that you can always ask generative AI for help. For example, you can tell Claude.ai or Copilot to *write Python code to open a json file named whatever.json, loop through its contents, and handle any exceptions.* Then just adapt the code it writes to your immediate needs.

Converting an Excel date to a JSON date

You may be thinking "Hey, waitaminit . . . what's with those 40554, 40950, 37683 numbers in the Date Joined column?" Well, those are serial dates, but you can convert them to Python dates. You'll need to import the xlrd (Excel reader) and datetime modules. Your first step will be to install that module, which you do by entering the following command in the VS Code Terminal window:

```
pip install xlrd
```

We talk more about modules and pip install in Book 4. But for now, the preceding command will get you started with this app. In your Python app, to convert that integer in the p['Date Joined'] column to a Python date, use this code:

```
y, m, d, h, i, s = xlrd.xldate_as_tuple(p['Date
    Joined'],0)
joined = dt.date(y, m, d)
```

To display this date in a familiar format, use an f-string, like this:

```
print(f"{joined:%m/%d/%Y}")
```

Here is all the code, including the necessary imports at the top of the file:

```
import json, xlrd
import datetime as dt
# This is the Excel data (no keys)
filename = 'people_from_excel.json'
# Open the file (standard file open stuff)
with open(filename, 'r', encoding='utf-8',
    newline='') as f:
    # Load the whole json file into an object
    named people
    people = json.load(f)

# Dictionaries are in a list, loop through and
    display each dictionary.
for p in people:
    name = p['Full Name']
    byear = p['Birth Year']
    # Excel date pretty tricky, use xlrd module.
    y, m, d, h, i, s = xlrd.xldate_as_
    tuple(p['Date Joined'], 0)
    joined = dt.date(y, m, d)
    balance = '$' + f"{p['Balance']:,.2f}"
    print(f"{name:<22} {byear}  {joined:%m/%d/%Y}
    {balance:>12}")
```

Here is the output, which is neatly formatted and looks more like the original Excel data than the JSON data. If you need to display the data in *dd/mm/yyyy* format, change the pattern in the last line of code to %d/%m/%Y.

```
Angst, Annie          1982  01/11/2011
   $300.00
Bónañas, Barry        1973  02/11/2012
   $-123.45
Schadenfreude, Sandy  2004  03/03/2003
   $0.00
Weltschmerz, Wanda    1995  04/24/1994
   $999,999.99
Malaise, Mindy        2006  05/05/2005
   $454.01
O'Possum, Ollie       1987  07/27/1997
   $-1,000.00
Pusillanimity, Pamela 1979  08/08/2008
   $12,345.67
```

Loading unkeyed JSON from a Python string

The load() method we used in the previous examples loaded the
JSON data from a file. However, because JSON data is always delivered in a text file, you can copy and paste the entire thing into a
Python string. Typically, you give the string a variable name and
set it equal to some triple-quoted string (like a Python docstring)
that starts and ends with triple quotation marks. Put all the JSON
data inside the triple quotation marks as in the following code. To
keep the code short, we've included data for only a few people, but
at least you can see how the data is structured:

```
import json
# Here the JSON data is in a big string named
   json_string.
# It starts with the first triple quotation marks
   and extends
# down to the last triple quotation marks.
json_string = """
{
"people": [
    {
    "Full Name": "Angst, Annie",
    "Birth Year": 1982,
    "Date Joined": "01/11/2011",
```

```
    "Is Active": true,
    "Balance": 300
    },
    {
    "Full Name": "Schadenfreude, Sandy",
    "Birth Year": 2004,
    "Date Joined": "03/03/2003",
    "Is Active": true,
    "Balance": 0
    }
  ]
}
"""
```

Seeing all the data from within your code like this might be nice, but there is one big disadvantage: You can't loop through a string to get to individual items of data. If you want to loop through, you need to load the JSON data from the string into an object. To do this, use json.loads() (where the s in loads is short for *from string*), as in the following code. That peep_data is a name we made up to differentiate the loaded JSON data from the data in the string:

```
# Load JSON data from the big json_string string.
peep_data = json.loads(json_string)
```

Now that you have an object (peep_data), you can loop through and work with the code one bit at a time, like this:

```
# Now you can loop through the peep_data
  collection.
for p in peep_data['people']:
    print(p["Full Name"], p["Birth Year"], p["Date
  Joined"],
          p['Is Active'],p['Balance'])
```

Figure 11-4 shows all the code and the result of running that code in VS Code.

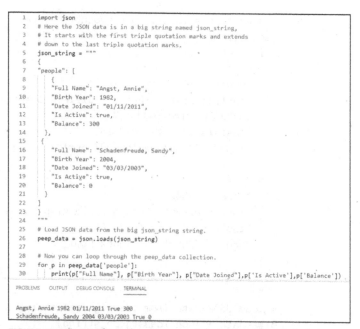

```
1   import json
2   # Here the JSON data is in a big string named json_string,
3   # It starts with the first triple quotation marks and extends
4   # down to the last triple quotation marks.
5   json_string = """
6   {
7   "people": [
8       {
9       "Full Name": "Angst, Annie",
10      "Birth Year": 1982,
11      "Date Joined": "01/11/2011",
12      "Is Active": true,
13      "Balance": 300
14      },
15      {
16      "Full Name": "Schadenfreude, Sandy",
17      "Birth Year": 2004,
18      "Date Joined": "03/03/2003",
19      "Is Active": true,
20      "Balance": 0
21      }
22  ]
23  }
24  """
25  # Load JSON data from the big json_string string.
26  peep_data = json.loads(json_string)
27
28  # Now you can loop through the peep_data collection.
29  for p in peep_data['people']:
30      print(p["Full Name"], p["Birth Year"], p["Date Joined"],p['Is Active'],p['Balance'])
```

PROBLEMS   OUTPUT   DEBUG CONSOLE   TERMINAL

Angst, Annie 1982 01/11/2011 True 300
Schadenfreude, Sandy 2004 03/03/2003 True 0

FIGURE 11-4: Output from showing one value at a time from each dictionary (see bottom of image).

Loading keyed JSON data from a Python string

You can store not only unkeyed data but also keyed data in a Python string. In the following example, we use json_string as the variable name again, but the data inside the string is structured differently. The first item has a key of 1 and the second item has a key of 2. But again, the code uses json.loads(json_string) to load this data from the string into a JSON object:

```
import json
# Here the JSON data is in a big string named
   json_string.
# It starts with the first triple quotation marks
   and extends
```

```
# down to the last triple quotation marks.
json_string = """
  {
  "1": {
    "count": 9061,
    "lastreferrer": "https://difference-engine.
  com/Courses/tml-5-1118/",
    "lastvisit": "12/20/2018",
    "page": "/etg/downloadpdf.html"
  },
  "2": {
    "count": 3342,
    "lastreferrer": "https://alansimpson.me/",
    "lastvisit": "12/19/2018",
    "page": "/html_css/index.html"
  }
  }
"""
# Load JSON data from the big json_string string.
hits_data = json.loads(json_string)

# Now you can loop through the hits_data
  collection.
for k, v in hits_data.items():
    print(f"{k}. {v['count']:>5} - {v['page']}")
```

The loop at the end uses two variables named k and v to loop through hits_data.items(), which is the standard syntax for looping through a dictionary of dictionaries. The loop prints the key, hit count, and page name from each item, in the format shown in the following code:

```
1. 9061 - /etg/downloadpdf.html
2. 3342 - /html_css/index.html
```

Changing JSON data

When you have JSON data in a data dictionary, you can use standard dictionary procedures (originally presented in Book 2, Chapter 4) to manipulate the data in the dictionary. As you're looping through the data dictionary with key:value variables, you can change the value of any key:value pair using this relatively simple syntax:

```
value['key'] = newdata
```

Removing data from a dictionary

To remove data from a JSON structure as you're going through the loop, use this syntax:

```
pop('keyname', None)
```

Replace 'keyname' with the name of the column you want to remove. For example, to remove all the lastreferrer key names and data from a dictionary created by the Firebase database JSON example, add the following to the loop:

```
v.pop('lastreferrer', None)
```

The None parameter in that code is optional. Including it prevents Python from throwing an exception if you try to delete a key that doesn't exist.

Figure 11-5 shows an example where lines 1–8 import Firebase data into a Python object named hits_data. Line 10 starts a loop that goes through each key (k) and value (v) in the dictionary. Line 12 converts the timestamp to a Python date named pydate. Then line 14 replaces the timestring that was in the lastvisit column with that Python date as a string in *mm/dd/yyyy* format. Line 16, v.pop('lastreferrer', None), removes the lastreferrer *key:value* pair from each dictionary. The final loop shows what's in the dictionary after making these changes.

Keep in mind that changes you make to the dictionary in Python have no effect on the file or string from which you loaded the JSON data. If you want to create a new JSON string or file, use the json.dumps() or json.dump() method, discussed next.

```
1    import json
2    import datetime as dt
3    # This is the Firebase JSON data (keyed).
4    filename = 'firebase_hitcounts.json'
5    # Open the file (standard file open stuff).
6    with open(filename, 'r', encoding='utf-8', newline='') as f:
7        # Load the whole json file into an object named hits
8        hits = json.load(f)
9
10   for k, v in hits.items():
11       # Convert the Firebase date to a Python date.
12       pydate = dt.datetime.utcfromtimestamp(v['lastvisit']/1000).date()
13       # In the dictionary, replace the Firebase date with string of Python date.
14       v['lastvisit']= f"{pydate:%m/%d/%Y}"
15       # Remove the entire last referrer column.
16       v.pop('lastreferrer', None)
17
18   # Now look at the lastvisit date in the hits dictionary.
19   for k, v in hits.items():
20       print(k,v)
21
22
```

```
PROBLEMS    OUTPUT    DEBUG CONSOLE    TERMINAL

-LAOqAyxxHrPw6pGXBHZ {'count': 9061, 'lastvisit': '12/20/2018)', 'page': '/etg/downloadpdf.html'}
-LAOQOxg6kmP4jhnjQKS {'count': 3896, 'lastvisit': '12/20/2018)', 'page': '/'}
-LAOrwciIQJZvuCAcyLO {'count': 3342, 'lastvisit': '12/20/2018)', 'page': '/html_css/index.html'}
-LAOs2nsVVxbjAuxUXxE {'count': 2220, 'lastvisit': '12/20/2018)', 'page': '/html_css/codequickies/'}
-LAOuq3sjfuoQx8WIS1X {'count': 2194, 'lastvisit': '12/20/2018)', 'page': '/index.html'}
-LAQ7ShbQPq0ANbDmm3O {'count': 1154, 'lastvisit': '12/16/2018)', 'page': '/javascript/code_quickies/'}
-LAQr56avlv0PuJGNm6P {'count': 1547, 'lastvisit': '12/20/2018)', 'page': '/how/'}
-LI0iPwZ7nu3IUgiQORH {'count': 1439, 'lastvisit': '12/20/2018)', 'page': '/datascience/beginner/'}
-LI2DFNAxVnT-cXYzWR- {'count': 1643, 'lastvisit': '12/19/2018)', 'page': '/datascience/cheatsheets/'}
```

FIGURE 11-5: Changing the value of one key in each dictionary, and removing an entire key:value pair from the dictionary.

Dumping Python Data to JSON

So far we've talked about bringing JSON data from the outside world into your app so that Python can use its data. Sometimes, you may want to go in the opposite direction, to take some data already in your app in an object (like a dictionary) and export it to JSON to pass to another app, the public at large, or whatever. This is where the json.dump() and json.dumps() methods come into play.

The dumps() method creates a JSON string of the data, which is still in memory, so you can use print() to see it. For example, the previous code examples imported a Firebase database to a Python dictionary, and then they looped through that dictionary, changing all the timestamps to *mm/dd/yyyy* dates and removing all the lastreferrer *key:value* pairs. So let's say that you want to create a JSON string of this new dictionary. You could use dumps like the following to create a string named new_dict, and you could also print that string to the console. The last two lines of code outside the loop would be

```
# Looping is done, copy new dictionary to JSON
   string.
new_dict = json.dumps(hits)
print(new_dict)
```

The new_dict string would show in its native, not-very-readable format, which would look something like this:

```
{"-LAOqAyxxHrPw6pGXBMZ": {"count": 9061,
   "lastvisit": "12/20/2018)", "page":
"/etg/downloadpdf.html"}, "-LAOqOxg6kmP4jhnjQXS":
   {"count": 3896,
"lastvisit": "12/20/2018)", "page": "/"},
   "-LAOrwciIQJZvuCAcyLO":
{"count": 3342, "lastvisit": "12/20/2018)",
   "page":
"/html_css/index.html"}, ... }}
```

We replaced some of the data with . . . because you don't need to see all the items to see how unreadable it looks.

Fortunately, the .dumps() method supports an indent= option, which you can use to indent the JSON data and make it more readable. Two spaces is usually sufficient. For example, add indent=2 to the preceding code:

```
# Looping is done, copy new dictionary to JSON
   string.
new_dict = json.dumps(hits, indent=2)
print(new_dict)
```

The output shows the JSON data in a much more readable format:

```
{
  "-LAOqAyxxHrPw6pGXBMZ": {
    "count": 9061,
    "lastvisit": "12/20/2018)",
    "page": "/etg/downloadpdf.html"
  },
  "-LAOqOxg6kmP4jhnjQXS": {
    "count": 3896,
    "lastvisit": "12/20/2018)",
```

```
    "page": "/"
  },
  ...
}
```

If you want to output your JSON data to a file, use `json.dump()` rather than `json.dumps()`. You can use `ensure_ascii=False` to maintain non-ASCII characters, and `sort_keys=True` to alphabetize key names. You can also include an `indent=` option, which can make the file more readable for human consumption. However, rarely use JSON to create human-readable files. JSON is primarily a marshalling format used to transport from databases to apps, and from apps to databases.

As an example, suppose you want to create a file named `hitcounts_new.json` (or, if it already exists, open it to overwrite its contents). You want to retain any non-ASCII characters that you write to the file. Here's the code for that; the `'w'` is required to make sure the file opens for writing data into it:

```
with open('hitcounts_new.json', 'w',
    encoding='utf-8') as out_file:
```

Then, to copy the dictionary named `hits` as JSON data into this file, use the name you assigned at the end of the code in the preceding line. Again, to retain any non-ASCII characters and, optionally, alphabetize the key names in each dictionary, follow that line with this one, indented so that it's contained in the `with` block:

```
json.dump(hits, out_file, ensure_ascii=False,
    sort_keys=True)
```

JSON is a widely used format for storing and sharing data. Luckily, Python has lots of built-in tools for accessing and creating JSON data. We've covered the most important capabilities here. But don't be shy about doing a web search for *python json* if you want to explore more.

Chapter **12**

Interacting with the Internet

s you probably know, the internet is home to virtually all the world's knowledge. Most of us use the web all the time to find information. We do so using a web browser such as Safari or Google Chrome. To visit a website, you type a Uniform Resource Locator (URL) into your browser's address bar and press Enter, or you click a link that sends you to the page automatically. This is the most complicated chapter in our book, but it is one of the most interesting to play with.

As an alternative to browsing the web with your web browser, you can access its content *programmatically.* In other words, you can use a programming language such as Python to post information to the web, as well as to access web information. In this chapter, you learn about the two main modules for accessing the web programmatically with Python: urllib and BeautifulSoup.

Seeing How the Web Works

When you open up your web browser and type in a URL or click a link, that action sends a *request* to the internet. The internet directs your request to the appropriate web server, which in turn sends a *response* back to your computer. Typically that response is a web page, but it can be just about any file. Or it can be an error message if what you requested no longer exists at that location. But the important thing is that you, the *user* (a human being), and your *user agent* (the program you're using to access the internet) are on the *client* side of things. The *server*, which is just a computer, not a person, sends back its response, as illustrated in Figure 12-1.

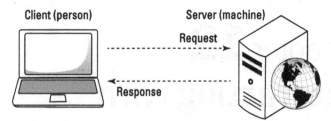

FIGURE 12-1: The client makes a request, and the server sends back a response.

Understanding the mysterious URL

The URL is a key part of accessing a web page, because that's how the internet finds the resource you're seeking. On the web, most resources use Hypertext Transfer Protocol (HTTP), thus their URLs start with http:// or https://. The difference is that http:// sends stuff across the wire in its raw form, which makes it susceptible to hackers and others who can "sniff out" the traffic. The https protocol is *secure* in that the data is *encrypted*, which means it's been converted to a secret code that's not as easy to read. Typically, any site with whom you do business and to whom you transmit sensitive information, such as passwords and credit card numbers, uses https to keep that information secret and secure.

The URL for any website can be relatively simple, such as Alan's URL, which is https://alansimpson.me. Or it can be complex, to add more information to the request. Figure 12-2 shows the parts of a URL, some of which you may have noticed in the past.

Note that the order matters. For example, it's possible for a URL to contain a path to a specific folder or page (starting with a slash right after the domain name). The URL can also contain a query string, which is always last and always starts with a question mark (?). After the question mark comes one or more *name=value* pairs, basically the same syntax you've seen in data dictionaries and JSON. If there are multiple *name=value* pairs, they are separated by ampersands (&).

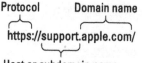

Protocol   Domain name

https://support.apple.com/

Host or subdomain name

https://alansimpson.me/python/cheatsheets/beginner/index.html

Path to folder and/or page

Query string

https://www.google.com/search?q=python+urllib+tutorial&tbm=vid

name = value   *name = value*

FIGURE 12-2: Different parts of URLs.

Exposing the HTTP headers

When you're using the web, all you care about is the stuff you see on your screen. At a deeper, somewhat hidden level, the two computers involved in the transaction are communicating with one another through *HTTP headers.* The headers are not normally visible to the human eye, but they are accessible to Python, your web browser, and other programs.

The product we use most often to view headers is HTTP Headers, which is a Google Chrome extension. If you have Chrome and want to try HTTP Headers for yourself, you can download and install HTTP Headers from the Chrome Web Store at `https://chromewebstore.google.com`. After you've installed the extension, to see the headers involved whenever you've just visited a site, click the HTTP Headers icon in your Chrome toolbar (it looks like a cloud) and you'll see the HTTP header information (see Figure 12-3).

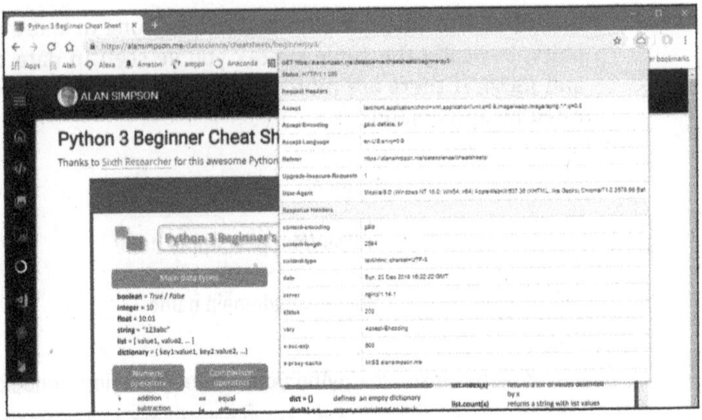

FIGURE 12-3: Inspecting HTTP headers with Google Chrome.

Two of the most important things in the HTTP headers are at the top, where you see GET followed by a URL. This tells you that a GET request was sent, meaning the URL is just a request for information; nothing is being uploaded to the server. The URL after the word GET is the requested resource. Another type of response is POST, and that means there's some information you're sending to the server, such as when you *post* something on Facebook or X (formerly Twitter).

The line below the GET shows the status of the request. The first part indicates the protocol used. In the example in Figure 12-4, the protocol is HTTP1.1, which just means the web request follows the HTTP version 1.1 rules of communication. The 200 is the status code, which in this case means "okay, everything went well." Common status codes are listed in Table 12-1.

All of what we've been telling you here matters because it's related to accessing the web programmatically with Python, as you'll see next.

Opening a URL from Python

To access the web from a Python program, you need to use aspects of the urllib, or *URL Library*, package. This one library consists of modules, each of which provides capabilities that are useful for different aspects of accessing the internet programmatically. Table 12-2 summarizes the packages.

GET https://alansimpson.me/datascience/cheatsheets/beginnerpy3/	
Status: HTTP/1.1 200	
Request Headers	
Accept	text/html,application/xhtml+xml,application/xml;q=0.9,image/webp,image/apng,*/*;q=0.8
Accept-Encoding	gzip, deflate, br
Accept-Language	en-US,en;q=0.9
Referer	https://alansimpson.me/datascience/cheatsheets/
Upgrade-Insecure-Requests	1
User-Agent	Mozilla/5.0 (Windows NT 10.0; Win64; x64) AppleWebKit/537.36 (KHTML, like Gecko) Ch
Response Headers	

FIGURE 12-4: HTTP headers.

TABLE 12-1 Common HTTP Status Codes

Code	Meaning	Reason
200	Okay	No problems exist.
400	Bad Request	The server is available but can't make sense of your request, usually because something is wrong with your URL.
403	Forbidden	The site has detected that you're accessing it programmatically, which it doesn't allow.
404	Not found	Either the URL is wrong or the URL is right but the content is no longer there.

TABLE 12-2 Packages from the Python urllib Library

Package	Purpose
request	Opens URLs
response	Handles the response that arrived; you don't need to work with it directly
error	Handles request exceptions
robotparser	Analyzes a site's robots.txt file, which grants permissions to bots that are trying to access the site programmatically

Most of the time you'll likely work with the `request` module because it enables you to open resources from the internet. The syntax for accessing a single package from a library is

```
from library import module
```

where `library` is the name of the larger library, and `module` is the name of the module. To access the capabilities of the `response` module of `urllib`, use the following syntax at the top of your code (the comment line is optional):

```
# import the request module from urllib library.
from urllib import request
```

To open a web page, use this syntax:

```
variablename = request.urlopen(url)
```

Replace `variablename` with a variable name of your own choosing. Replace `url` with the URL of the resource you want to access enclosed in single- or double-quotation marks (unless it's stored in a variable).

When running the code, the result will be an `HTTPResponse` object.

For example, you can run the following code in a `.py` file to access a sample HTML page that Alan added to his site for this purpose:

```
# Import the request module from urllib library.
from urllib import request
# URL (address) of the desired page.
sample_url = 'https://freeeasy.ai/sample.html'
# Request the page and put it in a variable named
    the_page.
the_page = request.urlopen(sample_url)
# Put the response code in a variable named
    status.
status = the_page.code
# What is the data type of the page?
print(type(the_page))
# What is the status code?
print(status)
```

Running this code displays this output:

```
<class 'http.client.HTTPResponse'>
200
```

The variable named the_page contains an http.client. HTTPResponse object, which is everything the server sent back in response to the request. The 200 is the status code that tells you all went well.

Posting to the web with Python

Not all attempts to access web resources will go as smoothly as the preceding example. For example, type the following URL in your browser's address bar, and press Enter:

```
https://www.google.com/search?q=python web
   scraping tutorial
```

Google returns a search result of many pages and videos that contain the words *python web scraping tutorial*. If you look at the address bar, you may notice that the URL you typed has changed slightly. The blank spaces have all been replaced with %20, as in the following line of code:

```
https://www.google.com/search?q=python%20web%20
   scraping%20tutorial
```

The %20 is the ASCII code, in hex, for a space. Those of you familiar with the web may recognize %20 because HTTP doesn't support the use of literal spaces in a URL. The %20 can be converted back to a space, if needed, after the transfer is complete.

Now take a look at what happens if you run the same code with the Google URL rather than the original URL. Here is that code:

```
from urllib import request
# URL (address) of the desired page.
sample_url = \
    'https://www.google.com/search?q=python%20
   web%20scraping%20tutorial'
# Request the page and put it in a variable named
   the page.
```

```
the_page = request.urlopen(sample_url)
# Put the response code in a variable named
    status.
status = the_page.code
# What is the data type of the page?
print(type(the_page))
# What is the status code?
print(status)
```

When you run this code, things don't go so smoothly. You may see several error messages, but the most important message is

```
HTTPError: HTTP Error 403: Forbidden
```

The error isn't with your coding. Rather, it's an HTTP error. Specifically, it's error number 403 for Forbidden. The URL was sent to Google, but it replied "Sorry, you can search our site from your browser, but not from Python code like that."

The good news is, sites that don't allow you to post directly using Python or some other programming language often *do* allow you to post content through their API (application programming interface). You can still use Python as your programming language. You just have to abide by their rules.

Scraping the web with Python

Whenever you request a page from the web, it's delivered to you as a web page usually consisting of HTML and content. *HTML* is markup code that, with another language called CSS, tells the browser how to display the content in terms of size, position, font, images, and all other such visual, stylistic matters. In a web browser, you don't see that HTML or CSS code. You see only the content, which is generally contained in blocks of HTML code on the page.

Even though much of the data you see on a web page comes from a database, you don't have permission to access the database directly. However, you can use a technique known as *web scraping* to pull data from the web page for use in some other manner. Python has great web-scraping capabilities, and this is a hot topic most people want to learn about. So we'll get started with web scraping using the sample page from Figure 12-5 as our working example.

FIGURE 12-5: Sample page used for web scraping.

The code that tells the browser how to display that page's content isn't visible in the browser, unless you view the *source code*. In most browsers, you can do that by pressing the F12 key or by right-clicking an empty spot on the page and choosing View Source or Inspect or some other such option. On most web pages, the real content — the stuff you see in the browser — is between the <body> ... </body> tags. Within the body of the page, there may be sections for a header, a navigation bar footer, perhaps ads, and more. In that particular page, the real meat of the content is between the <article> ... </article> tags. Each square that you see on the web page in Figure 12-5 is called a *card*, and each card is defined as a link in <a> ... </a> tags.

Figure 12-6 shows some of the HTML code for the page in Figure 12-5. We're showing code for only the first two links in the page, but all the links follow the same structure, and they are all contained in the section denoted by a pair of <article> ... </article> tags.

In the Python code, you need three modules. One of them is the request module from urllib, which allows you to send a request to the web for a resource and to read what the web serves back. That's one of the standard modules that comes with Python, so you don't need to acquire anything new for that.

For web scraping, you'll also want BeautifulSoup (whose name comes from a song in the book *Alice in Wonderland*). That module provides tools for parsing the web page that you've retrieved for specific items of data in which you're interested. Python itself doesn't come with Beautiful Soup already available, so you have to install it using pip. In VS Code, goes to the Terminal pane. If you're using Windows, enter this command:

```
pip install beautifulsoup4
```

```
60  <body>
61      <h1>Python 3 Cheat Sheets</h1>
62      <article class="cards256">
63          <a href="http://www.sixthresearcher.com/python-3-reference-cheat-sheet-for-beginners/">
64              <img src="images/basics256.jpg" alt="Python Basics Cheat Sheet">
65              <span>Basics</span>
66          </a>
67          <a href="https://alansimpson.me/datascience/python/beginner/">
68              <img src="images/beginner256.jpg" alt="Python Beginner Cheat Sheet">
69              <span>Beginner</span>
70          </a>
71          <a href="https://alansimpson.me/datascience/python/justbasics/">
72              <img src="images/justbasics256.jpg" alt="Python Just the Bascis Cheat Sheet">
73              <span>Just the Basics</span>
74          </a>
75          <a href="https://alansimpson.me/datascience/python/cheatography/">
76              <img src="images/cheatography256.jpg" alt="Python Beginner Cheat Sheet">
77              <span>Cheatography</span>
78          </a>
79          <a href="https://alansimpson.me/datascience/python/dataquest/">
80              <img src="images/dataquest256.jpg" alt="Dataquest Python Cheat Sheet">
81              <span>Dataquest</span>
82          </a>
```

FIGURE 12-6: Some of the code from the sample page for web scraping.

You should see some feedback on the screen indicating that BeautifulSoup was found and installed. Or, if you already installed it previously, you'll just see a message that the requirement has already been met. Nothing to worry about.

You will also need an HTML5 parser. You can use html5lib, which is another module you can install for free, right now. If you're using Windows, enter this command in VS Code's Terminal pane:

```
pip install html5lib
```

If you get an error using a Mac, use this command in VS Code's Terminal pane:

```
pip3 install html5lib
```

To try the code, create a .py file in VS Code and type the following code:

```
# Get request module from url library.
from urllib import request
# This one has handy tools for scraping a web page.
from bs4 import BeautifulSoup
```

Next, you need to tell Python where the page of interest is located on the internet. In this case, the URL is

```
https://freeeasy.ai/scrape_sample.html
```

To see the page, just enter the URL into your browser's address bar, as usual. In the browser, the page looks like any normal web page with some pictures. That's because the web browser shows the rendered page and not the raw HTML and CSS code. To scrape the page, you'll need to put that URL in your Python code. You can give it a short name, like page_url, by assigning it to a variable:

```
# Sample page for practice.
page_url = 'https://freeeasy.ai/scrape_sample.html'
```

To get the web page at that location into your Python app, create another variable, which we called raw_page, and use the urlopen method of the request module to read in the page:

```
# Open that page.
raw_page = request.urlopen(page_url)
```

To make it relatively easy to parse that page in subsequent code, copy it to a BeautifulSoup object. We named the object soup in our code. You'll also have to tell BeautifulSoup how you want the page parsed. You can use html5lib, like this:

```
# Make a BeautifulSoup object from the html page.
soup = BeautifulSoup(raw_page, 'html5lib')
```

TIP

Generative AI can write generic web-scraping code for you, so you don't have to memorize all the syntax. Just ask Copilot or Claude. ai to *write Python code to scrape a website using beautifulsoup.* That will get you the basic code for scraping a page. You then need to specify a URL and adapt the code to retrieve whatever you need from the page.

In the following code, we assign that block of code to a variable named content. Later code in the page will parse only that part of the page, which can improve speed and accuracy.

```
# Isolate the main content block.
content = soup.article
```

Storing the parsed content

When scraping a web page, your goal is typically to collect specific data of interest. In this case, we want just the URL, image source, and the text for a number of links. We know there will be more than one line. An easy way to store these is to put them in a list, so in the following code, we create an empty list named links_list:

```
# Create an empty list to hold a dictionary for
    each item.
links_list = []
```

Next the code needs to loop through each link tag in the page content. Each link starts with an ‹a› tag and ends with an ‹/a› tag. To tell Python to loop through each link individually, use the find_all method of BeautifulSoup in a loop. In the following code, as we loop through the links, we assign the current link to a variable named link:

```
# Loop through all the links in the article.
for link in content.find_all('a'):
```

Each link's code will look something like this, though each will have a unique URL, image source, and text:

```
<a href="https://alansimpson.me/datascience/
    python/lists/">
        <img src="images/lists256.jpg" alt="Python
    lists">
        <span>Lists</span>
</a>
```

The three items of data we want are as follows:

>> Link URL, which is enclosed in quotation marks after the href= in the ‹a› tag

>> Image source, which is enclosed in quotation marks after src= in the img tag

>> Link text, which is enclosed in ‹span› ... ‹/span› tags

The following code teases out each component by using the .get() method on BeautifulSoup to isolate something inside the link (that is, between the ‹a› and ‹/a› tags that mark the beginning and end of each link). The following gets the URL portion of the link and puts it in a variable named url:

```
url = link.get('href')
```

Indent that code under the loop so that it's executed for each link. The following code gets the image source and puts it in a variable named img:

```
img = link.img.get('src')
```

The text is between the ‹span› ... ‹/span› tags near the bottom of the link. To grab that text and put it into a variable named text, add this line of code:

```
text = link.span.text
```

You don't have to use .get() to grab the text because the text isn't in an HTML attribute such as href= or src=. It's just text between the ‹span› ... ‹/span› tags.

Finally, you need to save all that before going to the next link in the page. An easy way to accomplish that is to append all three items of data to the links_list using this code:

```
links_list.append({'url' : url, 'img': img,
    'text': text})
```

If data is missing, we prefer that Python just skip the bad line and keep going, rather than crash and burn, leaving us with no data. So we should put the whole business of grabbing the parts in a try: block, which, if it fails, allows Python to just skip that one link and move to the next:

```
# Try to get the href, image url, and text.
try:
    url = link.get('href')
    img = link.img.get('src')
    text = link.span.text
    links_list.append({'url' : url, 'img': img,
    'text': text})
# If the row is missing anything...
```

```
except AttributeError:
    #... skip it, don't blow up.
    pass
```

Figure 12-7 shows all the code as it stands right now. If you run it as shown, the link_list will be filled with all the data you scraped, but that doesn't do you much good. Chances are, you want to save that data to use elsewhere. You can do so by saving the data to a JSON file, a CSV file, or both, whatever is most convenient for you. In the sections that follow, we show you both methods.

```
EXPLORER                 scraper.py  ×
∨ SCRAPER2                  scraper.py > ...
   scraper.py            1   # Get request module from url library.
                         2   from urllib import request
                         3   # This one has handy tools for scraping a web page.
                         4   from bs4 import BeautifulSoup
                         5   # Sample page for practice.
                         6   page_url = 'https://freeeasy.ai/scrape_sample.html'
                         7
                         8   # Open that page.
                         9   raw_page = request.urlopen(page_url)
                        10   # Make a BeautifulSoup object from the html page.
                        11   soup = BeautifulSoup(raw_page, 'html5lib')
                        12   # Isolate the main content block.
                        13   content = soup.article
                        14   # Create an empty list to hold a dictionary for each item.
                        15   links_list = []
                        16
                        17   # Loop through all the links in the article.
                        18   for link in content.find_all('a'):
                        19       # Try to get the href, image url, and text.
                        20       try:
                        21           url = link.get('href')
                        22           img = link.img.get('src')
                        23           text = link.span.text
                        24           links_list.append({'url' : url, 'img': img, 'text': text})
                        25       # If the row is missing anything...
                        26       except AttributeError:
                        27           #... skip it, don't blow up.
                        28           pass
                        29
```

FIGURE 12-7: Web scraping code complete.

Accessing the web programmatically opens new worlds of possibilities for acquiring and organizing knowledge and is, in fact, part of a field of study called data science.

Chapter **13**

Libraries, Packages, and Modules

For the most part, all the chapters leading up to this one have focused on the core Python language, the elements of the language you'll need no matter how you intend to use Python. But as you've seen, many programs start by importing one or more modules. Each module is essentially a collection of prewritten code, which you can use in your own code without having to reinvent that wheel. The granddaddy of all this prewritten specialized code is called the Python standard library.

Understanding the Python Standard Library

The *Python standard library* is basically all the stuff you get when you get the Python language, including all the Python data types such as string, integer, float, and Boolean. Every instance of these data types is an instance of a class defined in the standard library. For this reason, the terms *type*, *instance*, and *object* are often used interchangeably. An integer is a whole number; it's also a data type in Python. But it exists because the standard library contains a class for integers, and every integer you create is an instance of that class and therefore an object (because classes are the templates for things called objects).

The type() function in Python usually identifies the type of a piece of data. For example, run these two lines of code at a Python prompt, in a Jupyter notebook, or in a .py file:

```
x = 3
print(type(x))
```

The output is

```
<class 'int'>
```

The output tells you that x is an integer and an instance of the int class from the standard library. Running this code:

```
x = 'howdy'
print(type(x))
```

produces this output:

```
<class 'str'>
```

That is, x contains data that's the string data type, created by the Python str class. The type() function works for a float (a numeric value with a decimal point, such as 3.14) and for Booleans (True or False).

Using the dir() function

The Python standard library offers a dir() method that displays a list of all the attributes associated with a type. For example, in the preceding example, the result <class 'str'> tells you that the data is the str data type. So you know that's a type, and thus an instance of a class called str (short for *string*). If you enter this command:

```
dir(str)
```

something like the following is displayed:

```
['__add__', '__class__', '__contains__', '__
   delattr__', '__dir__',
'__doc__', '__eq__', '__format__', '__ge__',
   '__getattribute__',
'__getitem__', '__getnewargs__', '__gt__', '__
   hash__', '__init__',
'__init_subclass__', '__iter__', '__le__', '__
   len__', '__lt__',
'__mod__', '__mul__', '__ne__', '__new__', '__
   reduce__', '__reduce_ex__',
'__repr__', '__rmod__', '__rmul__', '__setattr__',
   '__sizeof__', '__str__',
'__subclasshook__', 'capitalize', 'casefold',
   'center', 'count', 'encode',
'endswith', 'expandtabs', 'find', 'format',
   'format_map', 'index',
'isalnum', 'isalpha', 'isascii', 'isdecimal',
   'isdigit', 'isidentifier',
'islower', 'isnumeric', 'isprintable', 'isspace',
   'istitle', 'isupper',
'join', 'ljust', 'lower', 'lstrip', 'maketrans',
   'partition', 'replace',
'rfind', 'rindex', 'rjust', 'rpartition',
   'rsplit', 'rstrip', 'split',
'splitlines', 'startswith', 'strip', 'swapcase',
   'title', 'translate',
'upper', 'zfill']
```

Names surrounded by double-underscores, such as __add__ and __class__, are sometimes called *dunder-named* items, where *dunder* is short for *double underscores*. (Dunder-named items are often referred to as *special variables* or *magic methods*.) Each dunder-named item represents something built into Python that plays a role you don't necessarily access directly. For example, the __add__ method is invoked by using the + (addition) operator to add two numbers or join two strings.

The regular functions don't have the double underscores and are typically followed by parentheses. For example, take a look at these lines of code:

```
x = "Howdy"
print(type(x), x.isalpha(), x.upper())
```

The output is

```
<class 'str'> True HOWDY
```

The first part, `<class 'str'>`, tells you that x contains a string, which means that you can use any of the attributes shown in the output of `dir(str)` on it. For example, `True` is the output from `x.isalpha()` because x does contain alphabetic characters. `HOWDY` is the output of `x.upper()`, which converts the string to all uppercase letters.

TIP

Beginners often wonder what good seeing a bunch of names such as `'capitalize'`, `'casefold'`, `'center'`, `'count'`, `'encode'`, `'endswith'`, `'expandtabs'`, `'find'`, and `'format'` in a `dir()` output does for them when they don't know what the names mean or how to use them. Well, seeing the names doesn't help much if you don't pursue their significance any further. You can get more detailed information by using `help()` rather than `dir`.

Using the help() function

The Python prompt also offers a `help()` function with the syntax:

```
help(object)
```

To use it, replace *object* with the object type with which you're seeking help. For example, to get help with `str` objects (strings, which come from the `str` class) enter this command at the Python prompt:

```
help(str)
```

The output will be more substantial information about the topic in the parentheses. For example, whereas `dir(str)` lists the names of attributes of that type, `help(dir)` provides more detail about each item. For example, `dir(str)` tells you that there's a thing called `capitalize` in the `str` class, but `help(dir)` tells you a bit more about it, as follows:

```
capitalize(self, /)
    Return a capitalized version of the string.
```

```
     More specifically, make the first character
   have upper case and the rest
         lower case.
```

The word `self` just means that whatever word you pass to `capitalize` is what gets capitalized. The `/` at the end tells you that items listed before the slash are positional only, meaning that you can't use keyword arguments with them.

TIP

When you're finished viewing help, you don't have to scroll to the end to get back to the prompt. Simply press Ctrl+C.

When you do need more information and examples, the internet is your best bet. For example, you can use Google, Bing, or any search engine to search for the word *python* followed by whatever topic or function you're interested in. For example, searching for

```
python capitalize
```

provides links to lots of different resources for learning about the `capitalize` function of the `str` object, including examples of its use. If you're using AI, be it Copilot, Bard. ChatGPT, or whatever, you can ask for help and examples. For example try the prompt *tell me about Python str.capitalize()* or something along those lines.

A good (albeit technical) resource for the Python standard library is the standard library documentation itself. This information is always available at `https://docs.python.org/` usually under the Library Reference link. But even that wording may change, so if in doubt, just do a web search for *python standard library*. Be forewarned that the library is huge and technical, so don't expect to understand it right off the bat. Instead, use it as an ongoing resource to learn about things that interest you as your knowledge of Python develops.

Exploring built-in functions

Both `dir()` and `help()` are examples of Python built-in functions, which are always available to you in Python, in any app you're creating, as well as at the Python command prompt. These built-in functions are also part of the standard library. In fact, if you do a web search for *Python built-in functions*, some of the search results will point directly to the Python documentation. Clicking one of these results will open a section of the standard library documentation and display a table of all the built-in functions, as shown in Figure 13-1. On that page, you can click the name of any function to learn more about it.

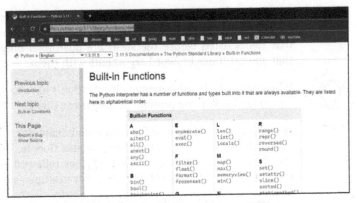

FIGURE 13-1: Python's built-in functions.

Exploring Python Packages

The Python language supports modular programming, in which a program is broken down into smaller, more manageable components, or modules. And some of those components might already have been created by someone else and can be reused.

Any large project, whether you're working alone or as a team member, can be simplified and streamlined if some components can use code that's already been written, tested, debugged, and deemed reliable by members of the Python programming community. The *packages* you hear about in relation to Python are that kind of code — code that has been developed and nurtured, is trustworthy, and is generic enough to be used as a component of a large project.

Thousands of packages are available for Python. A good resource for finding packages is *PyPi*, a clever name that's easy to remember and short for Python Package Index. You can check it out at https://pypi.org.

In addition, a program named *pip*, for Pip Installs Packages (another clever name) is a *package manager* that you can use to explore, update, and remove existing packages from your system.

To use pip, you have to get to your operating system's command prompt, which is Terminal on a Mac, and cmd.exe or PowerShell in Windows. If you're using VS Code, the simplest way to get to the command prompt is to open VS Code and choose View ⇨ Terminal.

If you already have pip, typing this command at a command prompt will tell you which version of pip is currently installed:

```
pip -version
```

If you're using a Mac and get a "command not found" error, you'll need to use pip3 in place of pip in all commands. For example, use

```
pip3 --version
```

The result will likely look something like this (but with your version's number, and the path to Python in place of the ellipsis [...]):

```
pip 23.1.2 from ...
```

To see what packages you already have installed, enter this at the operating system command prompt or in the VS Code Terminal pane in Windows:

```
pip list
```

Or on a Mac, use pip3 in place of pip if you get an error with pip:

```
pip3 list
```

Importing Python Modules

You'll hear the word *module* used with Python all the time. If you think of the standard library as a physical library and a package as a book in that library, a module is one chapter in one book. In other words, a package may contain many modules, and a library may contain many packages. The module is a big part of what makes Python a modular language, because code is grouped together according to function. You don't have to import everything including the kitchen sink to use *some* code. On the other hand, if you need to use several related things, such as functions for working with dates and times, you don't have to import them one at a time. Typically, importing the entire module will get you what you need.

You can import functionality from modules in a few ways. The way we just noted is one of the most common: import the entire module. To do that, just follow the import command with the name of the module you want to import. For example, the following command imports the entire math module:

```
import math
```

After you import a module, the dir() and help() functions work on that module, too. For example, if you tried doing dir(math) or help(math) before import math, you'd get an error. That's because that math package isn't part of the standard library. However, if you do import math first and then help(math), it all works.

There may be times when you don't need the whole kit-and-caboodle. In those cases, you can import just what you need using the following syntax:

```
from math import pi
```

In this example, you're importing one thing (pi), so you're not bringing in unnecessary stuff. The latter example, where you added "import pi", is also handy because in your code you can refer to pi as just pi; you don't have to use math.pi.

To see for yourself, at the Python prompt, such as in a VS Code Terminal window, enter the command print(pi) and press Enter. Most likely you'll get an error that reads:

```
NameError: name 'pi' is not defined
```

In other words, pi isn't part of the standard library, which is always available to your Python code. To use pi, you have to import the math module. You can do so in two ways. You can import the entire module by typing the following at the Python prompt:

```
import math
```

But if you do that and then enter

```
print(pi)
```

you'll get the same error again, even though you imported the math package. When you import an entire module and want to use part of it, you have to precede the part you want to use with the name of the module and a dot. For example, if you enter this command:

```
print(math.pi)
```

you get the correct answer:

```
3.141592653589793
```

Be aware that when you import just part of a module, the help() and dir() functions for the entire module won't work. For example, if you've executed only from math import pi in your code and you attempt to execute a dir(math) or help(math) function, it won't work because Python has only pi and not the entire module at its disposal.

You usually use help() and dir() at the Python prompt for a quick lookup rather than when you're writing an app. So using from is more efficient because you're bringing in only what you need.

You can also import multiple items from a package by listing their names, separated by commas, at the end of the from command. For example, suppose you need pi and square roots in your app. You could import just those into your app using this syntax:

```
from math import pi, sqrt
```

Once again, because you used the from syntax for the import, you can refer to pi and sqrt() in your code by name without the leading module name. For example, after executing that from statement, the following code:

```
print(sqrt(pi))
```

displays the following, which, as you may have guessed, is the square root of the number pi:

```
1.7724538509055159
```

You may also notice people importing a module like this:

```
from math import *
```

The asterisk is short for "everything." So in essence, that command is the same as import math, which also imports the entire math module, but with a subtle difference. Using the command from math import * automatically associates the names of constants and functions in the math module with that math module. So you don't have to use the math. prefix in subsequent code. In other words, after you execute the following:

```
from math import *
```

you can do a command like print(pi) and it will work, even without using print(math.pi). Although this approach seems smart and convenient, many programmers think it isn't Pythonic. If you're importing lots of modules and using lots of different pieces of each, avoiding module names in code can make it harder for other programmers to read and make sense of that code.

So that's it for Python libraries, packages, and modules. All three represent code written by others that you're allowed to use in any Python code you write. The only real difference is size. A library may contain several packages, a package may contain several modules, and the modules usually contain functions, classes, or other prewritten chunks of code that you're free to use.

Chapter **14**

The Ten Most Essential Aspects of Python

To be able program in Python is a very important skill for the modern worker in engineering, science, and business. So many of the new tools available for artificial intelligence (AI), data science, data analysis, and controlling equipment and robots all use Python. Python is rapidly become the programming language of choice. In this chapter, we fill you in on ten of the most essential aspects of Python.

Being Pythonic

The Python language is easy to learn but hard to master. The path to being fluent and effective in the Python language is one of practice. The more code you write, the better you become at writing code. In Python, it's not just making the program work that counts — it also matters how you do it. This is what we can being "Pythonic." If your Python code is hard to read and complicated, you aren't being Pythonic.

Python is designed to enable you to write clear code. Clear code isn't necessarily *concise* — it may have more statements — but the flow and intent of the code will be obvious.

REMEMBER

Beautiful is better than ugly. Explicit is better than implicit. Simple is better than complex. Readability counts. These are some of the rules for being Pythonic.

Identifying the Importance of Indents

Python uses indents to show control and structure in your code. Why indents instead of curly brackets? To eliminate redundancy (you were already indenting with curly brackets!) and make the code cleaner. Sounds very Pythonic to us! After a short while, using indents will become second nature to you.

TIP

Oh, and opening up a real source of contention, we suggest using spaces instead of tabs for indents! Make it a habit.

Understanding Python Syntax

The Python language has a very consistent flow of syntax through the entire language. Figuring out the basic syntax (see Chapter 3) will open up all the rest of the Python language in a natural way.

Appreciating the Flexibility of Python Variables

Python variables can contain almost anything. They aren't strongly typed as they are in C (you declare C variables as integers, for example). Instead, they're dynamically typed. In other words, a Python variable will be anything you want it to be. This information is important to remember when you're doing math on the variables — you can't add an integer to a string variable.

Seeing Lists as Your Friend

Lists are the most important compound data type in Python. They allow you to store and manipulate a whole collection of items at the same time. Understanding and using lists are key entry points into some of the most important applications in Python for AI, robotics, and data science.

Controlling Your Program

Programs in Python don't just run in one direction down the list of code. Programming applications require you to make decisions about what to do with your data (if statements), how many times to perform an operation (for and while statements), and how to move through all the data in your list variables.

Understanding Python Functions

Organizing your code and reusing pieces of Python code is very Pythonic and very useful to increasing your coding productivity and clarity. If you're doing the same thing multiple places in your code, you're better off putting the code into a function so if you need to change it, you only have one place to look. This approach also makes your code easier to read and maintain.

Figuring Out Errors

One of the most irritating aspects of Python for beginners is the relative obtuseness of the default error reporting in Python. Lucky for you, there are lots of methods for you to improve the readability of the errors generated by your code and to improve the readability of errors generated by Python itself. Understanding exceptions and errors will dramatically improve your Python experience.

Using Other People's Modules

Python would be nothing without the huge community of programmers who have generated modules that you can import into Python and use in your program. Tens of thousands of prewritten modules are available to help you out in your application. Need matrix math? It's out there. Need to manipulate images? It's out there. Want to try doing machine learning? It's out there. And most of the modules are well documented and easy to use.

Using the Web and AI When You Have Problems

Web searches and AI (such as ChatGPT and Microsoft Copilot) are your best friends not only when you're learning Python but also when you're actually developing applications. They're a great source of examples and documentation for doing specific tasks for your own applications. Use them. You aren't being replaced by AI tools — you're just getting to be more productive in your programming.

Index

Symbols

>>> prompt, 12, 14, 26

+ (addition) operator, 32

= (assignment) operator, 35, 40, 78

{} (curly braces), 87

/ (division) operator, 32

" (double quotation marks), 31, 34

== (equal to) operator, 33, 40, 64

> (greater than) operator, 33, 64

>= (greater than or equal to) operator, 33, 64

- (hyphen), 30

< (less than) operator, 33, 64

<= (less than or equal to) operator, 33, 64

* (multiplication) operator, 32

!= (not equal to) operator, 33, 64

% (percent sign), 49

+ (plus sign), 50–51, 79

(pound sign), 29

' (single quotation marks), 31, 34

[] (square brackets), 26, 78, 87, 134

- (subtraction) operator, 32

""" or ''' (triple quotation marks), 29

_ (underscore), 34

A

<a>...</a> tag, 156, 157

a (Append), 119

abs() function, 42, 43

action, operators for controlling, 63–64, 171

adding items to lists, 78

addition (+) operator, 32

AI (artificial intelligence), 7–8, 172

alignment, formatting, 49

alphabetize() function, 99–100

alphabetizing lists, 82–83

American Standard Code for Information Interchange (ASCII), 53, 151

and operator, 33, 64

Append (a), 119

append() method, 78, 84, 86–87

appending files, 125

application programs
    about, 27
    building, 27–40
    comments, 28–29
    data types, 30–32
    opening app file, 27–28
    opening files, 27–28
    operators, 32–33
    preventing crashes of, 110–111
    running in VS Code, 37–38
    saving work, 37
    syntax, 38–40
    variables, 34–38

arguments, passing arbitrary number of, 97–99

arithmetic operators, 32

<article>...</article> tags, 153

artificial intelligence (AI), 7–8, 172

ASCII (American Standard Code for Information Interchange), 53, 151

assignment (=) operator, 35, 40, 78

Auto Save, 18, 37

B

b (Binary), 119

base numbers, 49–50

bin() function, 43

binary files
    about, 117–118
    copying, 126–127
    reading, 126–127

<body>...</body> tags, 153

Boolean operators, 33, 64

Booleans, as a data type, 31–32

break statement, 70, 74

built-in functions, 43, 163–164

built-in help, 13–14

built-in methods, 54–55

C

About the Authors

John Shovic: John has been working with software since he talked his high school into letting him use their IBM 1130 computer for the entire summer of 1973. That launched him into his lifelong love affair with software. John has founded multiple companies: Advance Hardware Architectures; TriGeo Network Security; Blue Water Technologies; InstiComm; SwitchDoc Labs; and bankCDA. He has given more than 80 invited talks and has published more than 50 papers on a variety of topics on artificial intelligence, manufacturing automation, Arduinos, Raspberry Pis, computer security, computer forensics, embedded systems, and others. In 2019, he was appointed the director of the research group the Center for Intelligent Industrial Robotics. Currently, John is proud to be serving as a computer science faculty member, specializing in industrial robotics and artificial intelligence, at the University of Idaho in Coeur d'Alene, where he is surrounded by a bunch of students who are as excited about technology and computers as he is.

Alan Simpson: Alan is the author of more than 100 computer books on databases, programming, and web development. His books have been published throughout the world in more than a dozen languages and have sold millions of copies. Alan left the writing world a few years ago to get out of the ivory tower and into the real working world, first as a developer and now as a manager of the apps and DBA team in his county government's IT department. Alan has been called a "master communicator" throughout his extensive career, and his online courses and YouTube videos continue to get rave reviews from his many students and followers.

Dedication

John Shovic: To my wife, Laurie. She has supported me in so many ways including making sure my socks match in the morning, as well as keeping my PhD ficus plant alive. Thank you!

Alan Simpson: To Susan, Ashley, and Alec.

Authors' Acknowledgments

John Shovic: I would like to thank the wonderful staff at Wiley and give full credit to my co-author, Alan. Our technical reviewer, Rod Stephens, did an excellent and thorough job. Thanks to my literary agent Carol Jelen for encouraging me to pursue writing this book. I would like to specifically thank the University of Idaho for their support and suggestions, especially to Dr. Bob Rinker, Dr. Mary Everett, and Dr. Larry Stauffer. Great people, great university. Also, no book like this would be complete without my thanking my fabulous students, including James, Red, Garrett, Lacey, Jordan, Hunter, and Doug, who inspire me every day.

Alan Simpson: Many thanks to Steve Hayes and everyone else at Wiley for offering me this great opportunity. Thanks to Susan Pink, my intrepid editor. Thanks to my literary agents, Carol Jelen and Margot Maley Hutchinson of Waterside Productions. And thanks to my wife, Susan, for her patience while I was working at all kinds of crazy hours.

Publisher's Acknowledgments

Executive Editor: Lindsay Berg
Editor: Elizabeth Kuball

Production Editor: Saikarthick Kumarasamy
Cover Design and Image: Wiley